Praise f

Saving the World

'A rousing, feisty and fearless call to action for every one of us. Paola Diana entertains, cajoles and dares us to be the change that will enhance life for people the world over. A timely book and a compelling and provocative read.'

Shamim Sarif, novelist and filmmaker

'Having spent the last decade debating the business case for diversity, I thought I had a wide perspective of the issues but how wrong I was: Paola Diana, with her incredible book *Saving the World*, has made me think again and review the bigger picture as to the impact true equality of opportunity can have on society.'

Melanie Seymour, vice president of Women in Banking and Finance and head of BlackRock Budapest

'A powerful read... a must for all men! Strip us down and we're all equals; it's how we build ourselves up that counts! Ladies, your time is well overdue... break that mould, now over to you!'

Ant Middleton, adventurer, author, chief instructor on the Channel 4 series *SAS: Who Dares Wins* and captain on the adventure reality show *Mutiny*

'Paola's innate belief in the strength and absolute worth of women is contagious and uplifting and inspires you to embrace a new level of self-confidence without judgement. If you are looking for a non-intimidating and accessible snapshot of many of the challenges and opportunities for change, you should definitely read this book.'

Dr Sarah Caddick, neuroscience advisor to
Lord David Sainsbury

'All men should read this book, especially those who do not understand why discrimination against women is detrimental to society. *Saving the World* is a clearly stated case for removing all the barriers that prevent a woman's participation in every aspect of society. Women's full participation is good for business and good for society... Paola Diana shows us the way.'

David Stringer-Lamarre, entrepreneur and chairman of
the Institute of Directors, City of London

'I have never thought of myself as a feminist, however, I have now read Paola's wonderful book and realised that of course I bloody am!'

Fru Hazlitt, Channel 4 board member
and former MD of ITV

'For insights about the still unacknowledged power of women, *Saving the World* is the book to read. Paola Diana deftly details how equality can be reached, outlining the process in practical and economic terms. Cycles, from fashion to economics, may move swiftly but, as Paola Diana points out, gender roles and the accompanying limitations shift at an agonisingly slow place. Her insights will accelerate the process.'

Shelley von Strunckel, spiritual teacher and astrologer

SAVING THE WORLD

Women: The Twenty-First Century's Factor for Change

PAOLA DIANA

QUARTET

Originally published by Castelvecchi under the title *La salvezza del mondo. Donne: fattore di cambiamento del XXI secolo* in Italy in 2016

First published in Great Britain in 2018 by Quartet Books Limited
A member of the Namara Group
27 Goodge Street, London, W1T 2LD

Copyright © Paola Diana 2018

The moral right of the author
has been asserted by her in accordance with the
Copyright, Designs and Patents Act, 1988

All rights reserved.

No part of this publication may be reproduced, stored in a retrieval
system, or transmitted in any form or by any means, without the
prior permission in writing of the publisher, nor be otherwise circu-
lated in any form of binding or cover other than that in which it is
published and without a similar condition including this condition
being imposed on the subsequent purchaser

Reasonable efforts have been made to find the copyright holders of
third party copyright material. An appropriate acknowledgement can be
inserted by the publisher in any subsequent printing or edition

A catalogue record for this book
is available from the British Library

ISBN 9780704374515

Typeset by Josh Bryson
Printed and bound in Great Britain by
TJ International Ltd, Padstow, Cornwall

To Edward and Sofia, the twin lights of my soul

CONTENTS

Foreword

Espedita Fisher

Women's condition is a complex and continually evolving subject. Publications end up either dulling the brilliance of the entire female universe or illuminating just a few fragments of what is an enormous cosmological mosaic. This book is a journey through history and across the planet, uniting the perspectives of all women. It is more than an essay and takes on a most daring challenge: saving the world.

I met Paola while climbing my own ladder of personal achievement. Paola helps women emancipate; she helps them stand on their own two feet. I was younger back then, writing about how faith can make you happy, and I was looking for a job. I wanted to know myself as a woman; not only as a writer and a mystic. Paola believed in me, enhanced my confidence and self-esteem, and widened my possibilities.

Years later, when I was an established writer and my first two books, *Clausura* and *Eremiti*, had been well-received by critics and readers, Paola was in the process of opening her own training school and she renewed her guiding relationship with me. I was still looking for myself and my own worth as a woman. She believed that, besides being an author, I could be a teacher and she assigned me twenty young women who wanted to specialise and enter the job market. I discovered who I was by acknowledging in my students what I had overlooked in myself and I encouraged them not to give up and to believe in themselves.

Successful people can dream of a better world for themselves and for others. They do not turn defeat into resignation and instead make their wishes come true. They can create well-being around them, provide opportunities, *equal opportunities*. They can counteract the defeatist thinking of an economic crisis which has in turn become a human crisis. Paola is like that; she leads you towards a better life. You meet her and you do not regret living in Italy: you feel like you inhabit the centre of the world, and working for her you see what it is like to have your personal and professional rights respected; you feel valued and properly paid.

I have been following my dream career since I was eighteen years old, overcoming many obstacles and doing several other jobs to support myself in the process. All the while I never gave up on my vocation as a writer and a researcher: I believe in a better world where we all can fulfil ourselves. During a fundamental leg of my journey, I met Paola Diana. I hope she will sit here, beside me in my train car of goodwill, until the last stop. It was during another important leg of the journey that I read this book. It will stay in my heart's bookcase to be used as a reference forever.

Saving the World opens up the border between men and women. It is a book that inspires you to understand and improve yourself. It allows you to rediscover the cultural, social and political roots that have formed the gender gap. It is a book thinking ahead to the future. It sows the seeds of a more equal world, in which justice and equality rule professional and human relationships. It is a catalyst for confidence and goodwill and it is these qualities which allow the author to stand up to the world and uphold her integrity as a woman, a mother and an entrepreneur.

FOREWORD

I recommend this book to all those who wonder about economic and social inequality, about the destiny of women and the future of our planet which has been subjected to a man's game, lost from the start. Victory means equal opportunities. Above and beyond party politics and electioneering, equal opportunities will allow both genders to look at each other, respect one another and cooperate to save humankind.

Introduction

Domenico de Masi

Saving the World. Karl Marx's brilliant idea was that the working classes, by saving themselves, would save the world. At least in part, the working classes succeeded. The main idea of Paola Diana's fascinating book is that women, by saving themselves, will save the whole world. They are most likely to succeed.

In 2030, women will live three years longer than men. In the United States they will control two-thirds of all wealth. 60 per cent of university students, 60 per cent of graduates and 60 per cent of Master's degree holders will be women. Many women will marry younger men. Many women will have a child without a husband, whereas men will not be able to have a child without a wife yet. This is why women will be at the core of our social system and therefore potentially tempted to manage power with the toughness that comes from all the wrongs they have suffered during the previous ten thousand years.

Such certainties are the *arrière-pensée* of Paola's book, which tackles four key issues – women and politics, women and religion, women and work, women and society – and adds a draft bill proposing a tax intervention for women's entry and permanence in the job market: Bonus Care.

Paola's strong ideas, far from being utopian or odd, are precisely shared and confirmed by the conclusions of some foresight research which I have just completed. The objective of the survey was to verify how our social system will change from now until 2030. Using the Delphi method, I consulted eleven illustrious experts who agreed with the following summarised statements in terms of women's condition.

As for equality, the differences between women and men will reduce both in material (thanks to new, less physical and 'male' forms of employment) and symbolic as well as existential terms (for example on a sexual level). As time goes by, on the whole, our ethological (as animals) and social (as non-isolated human beings) mechanisms will be stronger than gender differences. Polymorphism and sexual fluidity, integrated into culture and law, will turn the tables as a mutation factor messes up the replication mechanisms of our genetic code.

By 2030, progress will be made towards equality by legislative measures aimed at gender balance, attention given to reconsidering vocabulary and language and provisions to protect women from violence suffered inside and outside the family at the hands of men. Such steps towards equality will be taken by accepting the current neoliberal framework, hence limiting the impact of these improvements. The two sexual cultures will continue to blend thanks to the growth of new genders, attributable neither to the male nor the female dichotomy. However, the endurance of the culture so far perceived as dominant will produce new forms of reaction and the possibility of male violence.

Clear distinctions will be perceived in areas of mainly male or female interest only (e.g. football for men, cosmetics for women). However, overall there will be many more areas of common interest in which culture represents a fair balance between the two approaches. The feminine point of view will take some time to assert itself in a male-dominated culture and women will need to deal with the danger of being integrated into the dominant model, in particular during the stages of climbing the ladder and subsequent power preservation.

Some jobs will continue to be mostly done by women (social services), others by men (jobs where physical strength is required) but the number of women holding responsibilities in top positions will increase. Women will enter sectors where their presence is currently rather low (for example, some scientific research areas), though top positions will continue to be mainly held by men.

As far as education is concerned, from now until 2030, family members will keep behaving according to the gender each is addressed by. But within the family, women will be able to exercise the right to express themselves with an increasing degree of equality. There will still be problems arising from new types of family, as a result of the expression of pre-existing cultures and religions placing women in a subordinate position in comparison with men.

On equal terms in regard to social, cultural and economic conditions, as well as access to top positions, women will increasingly show the skills needed to grow and gain success within schools and professional environments. The current trend records a considerable increase within young women's schooling; in their willingness to pursue their education and to achieve better results as quickly as possible. This trend is going to grow in the next decade.

In the society of 2030, educational and gender differences will have lessened but male and female icons will remain. The differences between male and female conduct will still be taken into due account. In 2030, men and women's publications will still be largely separate. However, topics of mainly female interest will be more and more dealt with in men's magazines.

As far as values and culture are concerned, women's dominant values in 2030 will be a search for harmony, sharing, an acceptance of men's surrender, civil liability as a work procedure and a care for relationships. The preferred values of women's progress will deeply change men, eroding the privileges which used to be considered natural, inspiring and driving change.

Women have been able to draw attention to issues and values that will gain an increasingly central importance in the coming years; in particular, sexual versatility, the criticism of men's violence arising from the idea of owning women, the promotion of diversity and variety, the practice of 'caring for the other' (overcoming selfishness) and maternity outside of marriage. Women's greater incisiveness will increase the importance of feminine values within society, moving our attention towards beauty, reducing violence and creating a greater tendency for dialogue.

In 2030, women will have acknowledged men's weakness and will be ready to change the world. Forms of sexuality thus far considered deviant will be assimilated into mainstream culture and become normal. Women will be able to affect the different sectors of public life and will bring innovation in social and cultural, as well as professional, terms. The values of beauty, subjectivity and sensitivity commonly ascribed to women will spread and shape the culture of the future.

Journalism, literature, art, cinema, scientific research, teaching, spirituality, sport and politics will make space for women's culture. The greater number of women within social, cultural and political life will continue to help develop more considered policies in regard to social, educational and equal-opportunities issues, founding governments of peace and integration.

From now until 2030, the distinction between men and women's culture will continue to be a source of comparison, discussion and growth, in order to promote a respectful integration of mutual needs and of psychophysical, mental and operational possibilities.

Women's intelligence will tend to reproduce forms of competitiveness, exploitation and the exclusivity belonging to power in the absence of sexual discrimination, because men's hegemony has trained the female sex to use the same weapons to survive. In 2030, competitiveness will no longer be predominately a male value. In terms of social competitiveness, women will take on traditionally male features (aggressiveness, decision-making skills, careerism etc.) and will develop a new emotional as well as cultural structure.

Women and work. Paola Diana's book pays particular attention to the relationship between women and work. For two hundred years, entrepreneurs, managers, chiefs and consultants have almost always been men, whereas women have been segregated at home playing the ancillary role of vestal virgins. In the *Gotha* of organisational sciences, well-known women like Mary Parker Follett or Joan Woodward can be counted on the fingers of one hand. The exclusion of women from corporate management involves the dominance of a male approach within companies: supreme rationality, fierce competition, a military hierarchy, mass standardisation and the creation of boring environments. Excluded from the world of work where men used to celebrate their hegemony, during the industrial society women built up their own world focused on the cult of service, beauty, subjectivity and sensitivity. Many mothers have been accomplices to such segregation. Well-known feminist Germaine Greer wrote that male chauvinism is 'like haemophilia: it attacks men but is transmitted by women.' But today, in the post-industrial society, values such as competence, flexibility, open-mindedness and willingness to experiment and play the game have been added to those cultivated in their segregation and determine women's professional and human superiority, especially within the areas of beauty, media, education, well-being, tourism and public relations, where the number of women succeeding in reaching top positions is increasing.

Now, we need to understand whether female enterprises where women can establish their own autonomous power are better, different or worse than the male enterprises we have been used to. It is important to know if, when women rule, the radical values that men have always banned from the world of work can finally win; values such as solidarity, conviviality, devoting oneself, cheerfulness, sensuality, sensitivity, beauty, creative inactivity. Lea Battistoni argued that women have different modes of scientific knowledge and logic as well as different, innovative organisational skills to men. We need to understand how male enterprises can change according to such feminine virtues.

In other words, thanks to women, does the brutal law of the strongest finally begin to crumble? A law theorised by men, and imposed by men on men. Are women capable of freeing us all by freeing themselves, of reinventing their work, of better combining duties and resources, of strongly upholding the right to start more beautiful and human-like companies, of establishing a female work ethic built upon a taste for well-done things, on a sense of responsibility, on an attention to human relationships rather than to money?

In the last few years the number of women managers and entrepreneurs has slightly increased; has something revolutionary finally happened to prove women's leadership more creative, more beautiful and fairer than men's? Do female ways to face work commitments exist? Does the greater availability to change, to creation, to equality and to happiness attributed to women managers exist? Does a different relationship with power and an ability to reject the abuse of power and manipulation exist? Does a different relationship with work, experienced as a creative opportunity instead of due atonement, exist? Does a different attitude towards creative inactivity, as a fertiliser of ideas, serenity and balance, exist? Is there any hope that Eros, once expelled and castrated by men's penchant for strict organisation, can be recovered by female enterprises? Even men begin to hope that the answers to such questions are affirmative.

Other differences. Our post-industrial world does not only need to cope with problems related to the inequality between men and women. There are other issues of equal depth related to differences in age, skills, race, ethnic group, language, customs, religion, sexual behaviours. To save the world, women not only need to help themselves but other downtrodden elements of society too.

INTRODUCTION

Women step into business centres mainly as cleaners or secretaries; gay men and lesbians can access them provided they keep their sexual orientations secret. It is estimated that homosexual men's 'faceless presence' within Italian companies is three times higher than in the United States, where the issue has been legally addressed even in the military system. On 18 December 2010, the American Senate approved a law allowing declared homosexuals to serve in the armed forces, so ending the regime of 'don't ask, don't tell'. The law had been at the core of the American homosexuals' political agenda for years. President Barack Obama sent a notice to the mailing list of his supporters in which he said that he was prepared to sign the law as soon as it arrived on his desk, in order to bring an end to such discriminatory policy. He announced that gay men and lesbians serving in the army, brave Americans fighting for freedom, would not have to hide themselves any longer. One less entry in the list of a nonstop battle for civil rights.

As a result of this legislation, something has moved forward on both sides of the ocean, though Trump tragically struggles to turn the clock back. It is recommended, however, that instead of focusing solely on politics, to speed up such difficult steps towards equality we should tackle the practices of companies: it is not only fair but also convenient. School, family and the worlds of art, fashion and design have already taken significant steps forward, whereas companies stick to their historically underdeveloped behavior; ethically unfair, economically detrimental and organisationally odd.

Saving the World. Women: The Twenty-First Century's Factor for Change is a beautiful and useful book. We should be thankful to Paola Diana. Especially us men who, with a suicidal determination, linger on to defend a gender supremacy which lacks an objective foundation by now. Unhappy with such a ridiculous notion as equality, we continue struggling to place fierce force at the service of our erroneous superiority, to beat back the promotion of women's worth with our gender bias. Paola Diana will likely agree with Françoise Giroud's ironic wisdom when she says that gender equality will be achieved when even a mediocre woman can become the president of a bank. It has always been possible for a mediocre man.

Prof. Domenico de Masi is an acclaimed sociologist and an emeritus professor in the sociology of work at La Sapienza University, Rome. He is the author of numerous sociological essays, many of which are bestsellers in Italy and Brazil.

Preface

I was born into a traditional Italian family where the father took all the decisions and held the purse strings. I was deemed good when I agreed with him and bad if I had different ideas. My brother, the male offspring, was always right; he would in time inherit the family's assets and perpetuate our father's surname. Mine was a northern family, from Padua, but I could have been born in any other city: the dominant culture in the seventies was the same everywhere. Had I been born in the south, I would have enjoyed even less freedom.

I began to be a feminist as a child, when certain instincts I must have been born with started to develop. When I say 'feminist', I mean a person who abhors the injustice and discrimination so often directed at women and who fights on their behalf for equal rights and opportunities in a world where women are oppressed by men. Wearing a different label, I would have championed men's rights if I had seen men being discriminated against in the same way by women. I myself endured the sort of routine psychological, and even physical, violence which was taken for granted within a 'normal' family when I was growing up; if you had a strong character and thought your own thoughts, as a girl you had no means of self-expression, you had to lower your eyes and submit. When I was small I silently rebelled but as I got older I started to speak out, determined to raise my voice to help myself and speak for the millions of other women who endure violence of all kinds on a daily basis.

Thanks to my classical studies and my degree course in political science, I was able to gain an insight into the contemporary world by exploring the historical and cultural heritage that underpins it. In studying the influence of church and state on patterns of human behaviour, I became increasingly convinced that from the earliest times the worst injustice to have afflicted our society is the maltreatment and repression of women: girls, mothers and widows. Across the Western world, there have for centuries, through periods of progress and change like the Enlightenment and the Industrial Revolution, been redoubtable feminists who have dedicated their lives to the cause of women's emancipation and thereby brought about reform. However, there are billions of women who are still innocent victims of a violent and victimising male culture. We cannot abandon them to their fate.

This call to arms is not only to emancipated women everywhere but to all men of conscience too, because we are all responsible. Governments should adopt policies specifically designed to promote respect for women's rights worldwide. A new diplomacy is required; the achievement of justice will only be possible through the joint action of governments and international organisations. Women are the main drivers of change in this century; the fate of the world depends on their liberation and emancipation. A fairer and less confrontational society is possible if women are given a voice; if they are invested with the authority to change policies and alter the very way in which the power currently residing in obsolete male paradigms is exercised.

PREFACE

The concerted pressure of a critical mass of educated and economically independent women – women who have reached top positions in economics, science, finance and politics – brought to bear at this time of technological revolution will be crucial in creating a better world; the sort of world we want our children to live in and one where men will live more fulfillingly as well.

Nothing is impossible; we just need to have a vision of the future we want to achieve and to want it enough to make it a reality. Each one of us can make a difference in some small way by working towards it with determination and sheer strength of purpose.

For millennia the patriarchal system has been based on unfounded myths. When it collapses under the weight of education and scientific knowledge, a new era will dawn: the era of women; the era of empathy, compassion, knowledge and peace; an era in which the brain and soul will count for more than brute strength.

London, 21 November 2017

1
Feminist Diplomacy

'One woman in politics changes the woman; but many women in politics changes politics.'

Michelle Bachelet

Diplomacy is the art of dealing with issues of international politics in such a way as to foster collaboration between states and meet their common needs. Deriving from the Greek word *diploos*, meaning double, it relates to negotiation between equals with mutual respect for their differences.

In the fifth century BC, the Athenian dramatist Aristophanes wrote a comedy destined to make history. The play, *Lysistrata*, is set during the Peloponnesian War, an outbreak of hostilities between Athens and Sparta which oppressed Hellas for over twenty-five years, and in it Aristophanes approaches the subject from a new and revolutionary perspective – that of women.

Lysistrata, an Athenian woman who is worried that the war shows no sign of abating, summons female representatives of all the Greek city-states to a meeting. They are women just like her, women distraught that their husbands and sons are risking their lives in battle while they wait at home, anxious and lonely. Spurred on by Lysistrata, they decide unanimously that the war must end and peace be restored, but how can they persuade the Athenians and Spartans to sign a peace agreement? The solution is simple. Women won't give themselves to their men until the factions put an end to the conflict. In addition, they will live barricaded in the Acropolis of

1

Athens in order to prevent men from accessing the wealth necessary to continue the war. Despite many difficulties, Lysistrata and her companions do not give up and Athens and Sparta agree at last to sign the peace agreement.

This work of Aristophanes may seem a simple comedy but there is much more to it than that. If we consider the position Athenian women were in during the fifth century BC, we find that Lysistrata is a feminist *ante litteram*; decidedly modern in her belief in the strength and empowerment of women. By taking the initiative and rallying her companions, she manages to change history for the better, finally bringing peace to a civilisation torn apart by years of conflict.

A few years after the success of *Lysistrata*, Aristophanes returned to the subject with *Women in Parliament*. Once again, the protagonists are Athenian women asking to take charge of the Assembly in order to save their city, which has been ruined by men's mismanagement. Obviously, the men in power deny them permission, so the women decide to infiltrate themselves into the Assembly disguised as men. Once in, they will implement the first reforms; money and goods will be made available to all, with the distribution administered by themselves. Moreover, the choice of men with whom to lie will be theirs to make; women will be free to manage 'their own bodies and lives' however they wish. An unimaginable concept for that time!

Aristophanes endowed his characters with some of the most fundamental attributes of femininity: innate wisdom, belief in dialogue and care for the weak. The women in his plays do not use violence to get what they want; rather they seek to negotiate an agreement. Moreover, when they fail in that, their reaction is never wicked or violent, but always firm and calm at the same time. Therefore, surely if dialogue, wisdom and the spirit of sacrifice are in short supply, the time has come for women, as in an Aristophanes's play, to exercise the art for which they are so ideally suited: diplomacy.

Economic requirements have now taken precedence over all others and have actually come to determine the relations between states. No country, except Sweden, has ever thought of putting aside these lesser needs in favour of more vital issues like the rights and dignity of women. For centuries, political and diplomatic power has been in the hands of men. Male culture defines the mores and manners of most societies and the freeing of women from this subjugation is unsurprisingly at the bottom of any list of priorities wherever men are in government.

In Sweden, where indeed a woman has been appointed minister of foreign affairs, a first attempt at what might be called 'humanitarian and feminist diplomacy' has been made. In February 2015, Minister Margot Wallström described the conditions of women in Saudi Arabia as 'medieval'. This is a widespread opinion in the Western world, but Saudi Arabia is a rich and influential country and states all over the world have a vested interest in maintaining good relations with it. This is precisely the drama of our time: on the altar of money and realpolitik we are sacrificing the lives and dignity of billions of women. Of course, the reaction of Saudi Arabians to the minister's statement was uncompromising: they immediately withdrew their ambassador from Sweden and explicitly accused Margot Wallström of being an enemy of Islam, thus implying that a sexist and discriminatory social system was in keeping with Islam. Sweden was left alone to manage the diplomatic crisis. What would have happened if the European Union, the United States, Canada, Russia, China, Japan and Australia had supported Sweden, insisting that there is no religious justification for female subjugation? Imagine a world in which every country changed direction in order to defend women of all nations. With new leadership, a new culture, a new *vision*, reform really could be achieved.

Feminist and humanitarian diplomacy should be based on the principle that women's rights are inalienable universal rights and, as such, cannot be denied because of religion, culture or tradition. As declared by Malala, the young Pakistani activist and winner of the Nobel Peace Prize, 'Traditions have been created by men and, if they are unjust, men can and should change them.'

Government action on behalf of women is imperative: the violation of their rights is the gravest and most widespread injustice in human history, and it is a legacy that, in our century, we still cannot rid ourselves of. Firm rejection of outmoded attitudes will ultimately lead to a better society, where the rights of children and minorities will be protected: this is what already happens in countries where women enjoy the same rights as men.

By its very nature, macho culture is characterised by discrimination, violence and abuse. We need to act against it. Europe itself, in view of its famed enlightenment, should be the standard bearer in this battle for civilization. A new politics where economic aid to countries is consequent upon their record of respect for women's rights must be the basis for this international diplomacy. If developing countries had to guarantee equal rights and dignity to women in order to have access to aid, the status of women in those countries would improve considerably. There is nothing to prevent the introduction of such measures apart from tradition, and that, as we know, can be changed. It is only a matter of will. We just have to want it.

Another objective of this new politics would be the provision of financial support for the associations that are fighting for democracy and for the protection of human rights in developing countries. It is a simple, pragmatic and effective approach. Every day, thousands of women fight without any means or voice to improve the society in which they live. By helping them, we would speed up internal processes of democratisation in those countries.

One example among many is that of Pakistani Syeda Ghulam Fatima, head of the Bonded Labour Liberation Front. This association has long been fighting for workers in Lahore's brick factories, workers who are often children living in conditions of virtual slavery. For years Fatima was left alone to combat this barbarism. She was beaten, threatened and even shot at. Eventually, an American blogger named Brandon Stanton, founder of Humans of New York (HONY), became aware of her plight and posted her picture asking readers to help. In less than seventy-two hours, Fatima received two million dollars for her cause. Stanton actively informed his followers just how best they could help those, like Fatima, already fighting for the rights of the slaves in Lahore.

If an individual like Brandon Stanton, certainly influential, but still an ordinary citizen, succeeded so impressively in his efforts, what could dozens of states do if they moved in this direction? What goals could be achieved by these heroic women standing up for human rights and risking their own lives? They would be able to change the world. Public opinion regarding human rights recently made progress thanks to the #FreeThe20 humanitarian campaign, conceived and carried out by the US government through Samantha Power, the young former US ambassador to the UN. The government demanded the release of twenty political prisoners across the world. 'In nominating them,' says Samantha, 'we sent a message to their governments: if you want to enable women, stop imprisoning them. Do not deprive your society and the world of their voices.'

The #FreeThe20 campaign has strong media value. It aims at shedding light on the stories of political activists who have spent their lives fighting, not only for women's rights but for the rights of all human beings, and have been deprived of their liberty as a result. The prisoners are just twenty but this campaign, the first based on a gender issue, seeks to put pressure on the offending governments to act in defence of human rights. The initiative was launched in the twentieth-anniversary year of the historic Beijing Conference of 1995 on women's rights and in anticipation of the Global Leaders' Meeting on Gender Equality and Women's Empowerment. Not surprisingly, the first of the twenty prisoners is Wang Yu, a forty-four-year-old Chinese lawyer guilty of defending women unjustly imprisoned, women that no other lawyer had the courage to defend. She was imprisoned, along with her husband and her sixteen-year-old son, and subjected to violence, threats and attacks on her reputation. The US government pointed the finger at China for this serious violation of human rights. What will other Western democracies do? Will they ignore the violation or will they speak out for Wang Yu and all prisoners like her? We know that pressure from political groups and from the international media can do much to free prisoners worldwide. Let us make use of these forces to save women.

The continuing evolution of the human species requires political and social systems to be replaced by more advanced models when they become less effective. It's time to change: we must have no more politics based on power, but instead the creation of a space in which to chart new paths of development for society's benefit and welfare. The ultimate goal should be the happiness of citizens. This vision can never be made a reality by the sort of traditional politics that are still very much tied to a patriarchal capitalist concept of society. Nevertheless, as Lysistrata and her companions demonstrated, women around the world can always resort to revolution.

It is important here to reflect briefly on the word 'feminist' and its implications. Very often, negative connotations are undeservedly attached to the term. In discussing the subject with a Member of the Italian Parliament of my acquaintance, I was confirmed in my belief that there is considerable confusion as to the actual meaning of the word. In commenting on yet another case of violence towards a woman, I said it would be nice if, after death, there was a feminist paradise where the souls of all women could find peace for themselves. He agreed that it would be nice for them, just as a 'macho' paradise would be nice for men. Looking at him in astonishment, I explained that there is a huge difference between the two terms: being a feminist doesn't mean being against someone; it is rather about promoting respect for women's rights. Being 'macho', on the other hand, means rejecting equality of rights between the genders.

'Feminism' is virtually a synonym for parity and equality. A man who believes in the values of freedom and fairness can himself be thought of as a 'feminist'. Machismo, on the other hand, champions male primacy in support of a patriarchal society. If this simple distinction is not clear to a representative of the state, I thought, whatever must be the understanding of most of the population? Historically, feminists have been hostile and even violent towards men on occasions, but this was only when men had sought to perpetuate a culture of oppression and violence. We owe much to the women who fought against all odds for those rights, such as votes for women, that we now take for granted.

Today there is little overt conflict between the genders. Indeed, the fact that we can only help the cause of equality by working together is widely recognised. In this regard, the HeForShe campaign promoted by the UN is emblematic. It is an initiative aimed at emphasising the need for the active and unreserved support of all men in favour of gender equality – the ones I like to call 'enlightened'.

Gender equality is not just a female issue: it should be of great concern to all human beings who aspire to a more just society. Therefore, it is important that we women do not just discuss these matters among ourselves. It is precisely with the men close to us – fathers, husbands and sons – that we should talk. Only then can we achieve universal enlightenment in the field of human rights.

I would like this little book to be read by you, female friends, and given to as many men as you know, so that at least one or two seeds may take root and sprout equality. If you are mothers, you have also the responsibility of raising mindful and respectful sons so that they become better men. Do not forget: if we have given birth to generations of men who denied us any rights, it means that part of the blame is down to our nurturing. It all begins with dignity and respect.

History of the female condition: a history in half

Until recently, nobody ever, to my knowledge, wrote history books presenting the past from a female point of view. As an academic subject, history has always been the preserve of men, who over the centuries have told the past in their own way. There have been remarkable women – queens like Elizabeth I, for example, who brought prosperity and stability to their nations – but on the whole the history of mankind is full of wars and acts of violence perpetrated by male rulers.

Imagine if, from the Middle Ages to the present day, half the nations in Europe and Asia had been led by strong and emancipated women; never oppressed by cultural and religious dictates, able to express their natural wisdom and humanity. Would there have been the same wars? The same slavery? Would millions of people have been exterminated? Obviously, these women would not have limited power to themselves: they would have appointed other women to senior positions in all fields, from law to art.

90 per cent of the world's ambassadors are men. Yet it is generally agreed that the female gender is more skilful at diplomacy than the male. And it goes without saying that a woman who gives life does not knowingly carry a child only to see it die in war a few years later. This is not her mission in the world! History would have been very different if women had from the outset been given

9

the opportunity to leave an imprint on international politics. In the words of Zainab Salbi, founder of Women for Women International, 'War has a male perspective. However, during a war we continue to live: eating, sleeping, going to school, working. And it is women who guarantee all this. The female perspective is the only one looking at peace.'

The English philosopher and economist John Stuart Mill describes very well the status of women throughout the centuries. At the end of the nineteenth century, Mill demanded to know how it was possible to establish from birth that women could not be employed in jobs that were legally open to stupid and cowardly members of the opposite sex.

This enlightened man, unsurprisingly married to feminist Harriet Taylor, explained how the millennial injustice suffered by women, like forms of discrimination based on religion or ethnicity, damages the cultural and economic development of a society, impoverishing the whole of humanity in the process.

If we think about women of the past, compelled to be subservient, first to the father and then to the husband, deprived of the right to study, work and vote, we see a vitiated society, where the privileges of the male caste are maintained through a social and political system that justifies all sorts of abuses. History does not necessarily repeat itself. Humanity needs to evolve and, for this to happen, it is necessary for women to stop being considered daughters of a lesser god.

For centuries, men with such capability have subdued and oppressed human beings of inferior physical strength. Along with their perceived lack of strength, women's intelligence was also believed to be inferior to that of men and therefore women were limited in their civil, political and social involvement. This discrimination has the bitter taste of racism. It is creeping, silent and, precisely for this reason, insidious. Today nobody shouts about women being less capable, intelligent or gifted, yet many people are still steeped in prejudice about such matters. And they act accordingly. Unfortunately, many of us do not realise this and become tolerant of damaging traditions. Think about genital mutilation and arranged marriages to so-called 'child brides': these are monstrous customs that are actually carried out by the mothers of the victims. Iranian lawyer Shirin Ebadi, winner of the Nobel Peace Prize in 2003, quoted Germaine Greer in observing that 'machismo is like haemophilia: it attacks men but is transmitted by women. Macho culture is undemocratic because it excludes women from political decisions. If a man thinks that the women of the house are worth less than him, it will follow that, in society, he will consider one elite entitled to decide for all.' To change the world, we need to overcome history, starting with our own family dynamics.

History of the female condition: historical overview

Man has always been obsessed with having control of the sexual sphere and, with it, the female body.

In ancient Greece men kept their wives – often as young as twelve years old – confined to the house, and habitually betrayed them with concubines or with a hetaera, a sort of luxury escort for the affluent. Greek society was unashamedly male-dominated. Demosthenes in 350 BC wrote that for the Athenians there were three different types of women: courtesans to have fun with, prostitutes to satisfy sexual needs and wives with whom to procreate. In short, in the Hellenic world wives existed only to serve their husbands and had no more rights than a slave. The entire culture was designed to indulge one gender at the expense of the other. For a man to have three women was perfectly acceptable but for his wife absolute loyalty and devotion were de rigueur.

This cannot but bring to mind the institution of the harem, so dear to the Eastern sultans and still in vogue in some countries today. Women in a harem are objects of pleasure, kept at the complete disposal of powerful men. Many of their male subjects would have liked to enjoy the same privileges as the sultans and some religions, such as Islam and the Mormon Church, have decreed that even men of lower class may have several wives at the same time, provided they are able to support them. Of course, the opportunity to have more than one husband was never granted to women.

Total control over female sexuality could be obtained through the use of a barbaric contraption called a 'chastity belt', a tool that physically prevented wives from having sex with anyone else when their husbands were absent. Dear male friends, you who are reading these pages, would you not have found it cause for revolution if you had been forced to such degradation?

In medieval times, two institutions emerged that characterised the history of the centuries to come: the monarchy and the feudal system. Both were based on the concept of nobility, a form of selection that rewarded the best warriors, or the heirs by birth of earlier warriors, by giving them power over others. Land, servants, women and beasts all became property of the warrior, who could dispose of them however he liked. By extension, the imperial system developed in a wider context geographically. The mechanism was simple: establish supreme power over everything and everybody and legitimise it by claiming rule by divine right, to the detriment of the helpless and submissive local population who are dominated through their ignorance and superstition. Within this system, the woman was isolated in the home and had designated tasks: to procreate and to take care of the house. Her social roles were those of daughter, wife and mother. The only alternative was the monastic life. At the time, it was easy to instil this culture in women, relying on their ignorance and naivety. This state of affairs is now consigned to the past in the Western world, but in many developing countries it still represents a sad present. No harassment is worse than having one's freedom of choice removed. A woman without control over her life is already doomed to unhappiness.

Unfortunately, the Renaissance did not bring marked improvements in the status of women. Indeed, it was precisely the revival of Roman law that worsened it even further: the first provision, depriving women of the right of succession, was enacted by Philip the Fair in 1317.

In the fifteenth century, another pretext for the persecution of women was found – the fallacious belief that some of them practised witchcraft. The victims were mostly educated and emancipated women, dangerous curiosities by the religious and cultural standards of the day. Prominent among Italian women accused of witchcraft is Laura Malipiero, arrested and tried several times for having cured, outside the medical profession, dozens of women in seventeenth-century Venice. Together with her mother Isabella, Laura practised the science of body and soul healing, surrounding herself with a strong network of women from all walks of life who were united in striving to advance their own area of knowledge.

In the seventeenth century, wives started to take their husband's surname, further associating a loss of identity with marriage. In Western countries, this custom has become optional, thanks to the Enlightenment, the Industrial Revolution and the teachings of Marx. In the East, history has taken a different turn, and the tradition continues.

During the Enlightenment, Paris was thought of as the global capital of culture. There, women became avid readers of novels and the concept of universal education gained ground. The Enlightenment, with the victory of reason over superstition, was the salvation of women. As Voltaire said, 'Witches have ceased to exist since we ceased to burn them.'

The Industrial Revolution brought another crucial shift in the development of the female condition: on the one hand it helped to release women from the home and enter the world of work but on the other the price they paid was very high. In the mines, women were used instead of horses since they were less expensive; they were harnessed, just like animals, and forced to drag heavy wagons.

When I hear girls making negative comments about feminism or laughing at it, I would like them to travel through time to see for themselves what it was like to be a woman before the feminist movement came to save us. I wish they could have a taste of life back then in order to understand what we owe to the brave women who defied imprisonment, violence, rape and death for us. Of course, today the word 'feminist' can be misinterpreted. Perhaps a campaign is necessary to raise awareness and disseminate information regarding its true meaning. Or maybe, we should just let things evolve, hoping that over time everyone will become 'enlightened'. Both men and women.

Among earlier feminist movements, the crusade of the Suffragettes has a place of honour. In England, in the early twentieth century, these women fought with strength and determination to get the right to vote, which until then had been denied them. Led by the indomitable Emmeline Pankhurst, who had founded the Women's Social and Political Union in 1903, the Suffragettes endured all kinds of abuse, repeated detentions and the violent repression of their peaceful demonstrations until they were forced to resort to drastic measures, such as hunger strikes, in order to gain visibility and to be heard by the politicians of the time. Their battle ended in victory when, in 1918, the UK Parliament agreed to grant the right to vote to householders' wives over the age of thirty. Universal suffrage was achieved ten years later. Spurred on by the success of the Suffragettes in Britain, women in Italy began a similar movement but it was destined to face formidable opposition. Not only were members of the Parliament determined to reject the proposed legislation but it was also up against the entrenched prejudice of women who did not wish to be emancipated. As Princess Cristina Trivulzio Belgiojoso, the Italian patriot and literary figure, observed, 'Those few female voices that have been raised asking men for formal recognition of their equality are opposed more by the majority of women than men themselves.'

15

The words of Giuseppe Mazzini, an enlightened man who did not hesitate to give his support to the cause of women's suffrage, are helpful in understanding the political climate that prevailed at the time: 'The emancipation of women would sanction a great truth, a basis for all the other ones, the unity of mankind, and would combine in the search for truth and common progress a sum of powers and forces rendered barren from that soul-halving inferiority. However, hoping to get the bill passed by Parliament in its present form, and in the current Italian establishment, is like being the first Christians and hoping to get from paganism the inauguration of monotheism and the abolition of slavery.' His words are still relevant today: until legislative power is in the hands of a critical mass of capable feminist women, the reforms needed to improve their daily lives, and consequently the lives of families and children, will not be possible.

Among the first Italian women to actively fight for the improvement of their condition was Rosa Genoni, a milliner known for having 'invented' the Italian style. She was the only delegate of our country to participate in the first conference of the Women's International League for Peace and Freedom in 1915. On that occasion, more than a thousand women met to discuss the ongoing war and the measures necessary to better their position throughout the world. The delegations sent to world leaders by the conference asking for the recognition of full civil and political rights for women were barely heard. Several years had to pass before the dreams of Rosa Genoni and her companions were finally realised.

In discussing those Italians who fought for universal suffrage, it is important to mention the feminist Anna Maria

Mozzoni. Her words are still relevant: 'The emancipation of women is the highest, largest and most radical social issue, capable of uniting women of all walks of life in the cause of freedom and redemption.' It took more than sixty years for the right to vote, a right we now accept without question, to be granted to Italian women. It was applied for the first time not so very long ago, in 1945, after years of debate and hesitation by those in power.

The sixties and seventies saw the development of a new feminism: the women of Europe and the United States claimed full rights over their own sexuality, rejecting outside interference of any sort. Even in Italy, activists filled the streets, finding spaces to congregate in the universities and other intellectual environments. Yet this, one of the greatest women's revolutions our country had ever seen, was triggered by a simple girl from a small town in the south: Franca Viola. In 1965, this young Sicilian girl was kidnapped and raped by the son of a local gangster, with whom she had recently broken off a relationship. At the time, both Italian law and common morality demanded a 'shotgun wedding' – the crime of rape could be quashed if the aggressor married his victim. Otherwise, the stigma would make it virtually impossible for the 'shameless' girl to find a husband. Franca Viola refused the shotgun wedding and became a symbol of courage and empowerment for the whole country. Three years after the rape, Franca married another man instead and married him for love.

How many of these women who have transformed our culture or made a contribution to humanity are remembered with busts, statues, squares or streets? Very, very few. They have not received the glory they deserve.

In a recent study of the extent of women's toponymy, it emerged that in Italy only 5 per cent of streets bear the names of women, often mothers of male celebrities. In Milan, it is as low as 3 per cent. These are paltry figures that speak for themselves.

What does it take to broaden the toponymy? What does it take to accord a fitting tribute to the memory of those who deserve it? What does it take to give our daughters recognition and our children a more balanced view of history? What are we waiting for? Memory nourishes the identity of a community. Without the past, there is neither present nor future, be it for an individual or an entire nation.

It may seem that our streets and squares being named after men is a minor matter, just a detail, but you should never underestimate details. That's where the devil lurks. Women have lived for centuries outside the sphere of history and politics. But they are not the only ones who have been deprived by this. The whole world has suffered from their absence.

Consider the scourge of totalitarianism. All the oppressors and dictators of recent history have been men: Stalin in the Soviet Union, Idi Amin Dada in Uganda, Pol Pot in Cambodia, Hitler in Germany, Pinochet in Chile. Their regimes relied on violence and discrimination. All were exemplars of choking, sapping, killing machismo.

If humankind is to survive and evolve it cannot ignore the plight of women in many parts of the world. It took centuries to recognise that racism and slavery are abominations. Similarly, we must realise that we cannot deprive the female half of the population its fundamental rights on the grounds that women are physically weaker.

We no longer live in the jungle; the law of the survival of the fittest no longer applies; the concepts of solidarity, piety and empathy should be the pillars on which we base our society. Only love can save us. In the words of the famous writer Erri De Luca, 'The male is envious of the female's power to give birth. He has carved for himself power in the areas of war, politics, government – but all are inferior in every way to the giving of birth to new life. In giving birth the woman reproduces the supreme work of creation. And now is "the time of mothers".'

The global socio-economic outlook

The status of women is a complicated subject, always avoided rather than addressed. Even philosophers like Aristotle and Plato never debated the issue. Even during the Renaissance, the rebirth of art and learning, women did not benefit from any change arising from the revision of thought.

Historically, women have been denied the right to education and, as a consequence, the right to most work. The daughters of the wealthier social classes could become respectable wives or nuns. Less fortunate girls were relegated to the most menial tasks, performed in inhuman conditions, or were forced to join the ranks of women who did the oldest and most degrading job in the world – prostitution. In the past, a woman was seen only in terms of her ability to procreate, to be devoted to the house with all that this implies. She was denied any form of expression, any access to art and culture. The segregation that women have undergone over the centuries has inflicted a deep wound on the whole of humanity and their exclusion from public life represents a missed opportunity for greater progress in every field.

One instance of a woman surmounting these obstacles is the case of Artemisia Gentileschi, daughter and student of the painter Orazio Gentileschi. She was raped by Agostino Tassi, a close friend of her father's. The trial that followed was terribly unfair: to confirm the reliability of the charge of rape, Artemisia was tortured. It took several months before the girl was able to paint again. Nevertheless, the drama and the anger she experienced became an integral part of her style, making her one of the most respected and renowned artists of the seventeenth century.

Today we live in a time of change in which freedom and love have become the keystones of a better future. A new, more just and peaceful, civilization is possible; though, for that to happen, we must put an end to the hegemony of men, to their rule and to the patriarchal culture that perpetuates it. First of all, we need to acknowledge the extent of it and *talk* about it, looking reality in the face. A profound and reasoned change is not possible without an objective analysis of this subject.

The status of women is a global issue; it touches every human being without exception. How is it possible that countries where women have achieved political, economic and social rights after exhausting struggles remain seemingly indifferent to the egregiousness of other nations where the plight of women is still tragic? The time has come to take a *leap* and help those left behind. Why this indifference? The lack of interest stems from two important and connected factors: public opinion with regard to the status of women is not strong enough to force lawmakers to fight for their rights, at home or abroad; and there are not enough women in political and economic leadership roles to act as standard-bearers for the campaign of reform.

These two factors are inextricably linked: one affects the other and vice versa. The only way to correct this state of affairs is for the 'enlightened' ones to discuss the problem as well, highlighting its origins and extent, looking for shared solutions in the creation of a code of universal values designed to protect women's rights and guarantee them the respect accorded to men. A revolution *inside* the male world must take place: only with the support of men can women empower themselves and understand the value they represent to society. Every woman must be enabled to live a full life, free from unseen obstacles, prejudice, violence and pain.

The status of women is the social and political barometer of a nation. The more rights and freedoms its women enjoy, the nearer it is to being adjudged a 'perfect' democracy. The more abuses and discrimination its women suffer, the more its politics are likely to be mired in authoritarianism and corruption. In the words of Hillary Clinton, from her historic speech in 1985, 'Human rights are women's rights and women's rights are human rights.'

In the course of rethinking diplomacy worldwide, we have to review the democratic model in Western countries. As we face growing tensions in the Eurozone, we must ask ourselves what is *not* working in this system. The kind of democracy in force in most states is closely connected to an economic model dominated by global finance at the expense of sustainability and general welfare. By changing the economic system in a spirit of solidarity and the sharing of 'typically female values' we may be able to enter a new era. A multitude of women leaders at local and national levels will finally have the opportunity to rethink a paradigm that at this point is no longer able to meet our aspirations. In this way, not only politics but also the whole economy will change. Even methods and modes of working may change. As the sociologist Domenico De Masi correctly points out, 'The exclusion of women from corporate management involves the dominance of a male approach within companies: supreme rationality, fierce competition, a military hierarchy, mass standardisation and the creation of boring environments.'

Innovative solutions, such as the spread of smart-working, could combine flexibility and productivity in the workplace and greatly improve the lives of both men and women, making them freer and happier.

2
God is a Woman

'You should change your attitude not your sky.'

Seneca

American President Jimmy Carter said that, 'The world's discrimination and violence against women and girls is the most serious, pervasive and ignored violation of basic human rights.' He maintained that it is due to the misinterpretation of religious texts that women are widely considered inferior to men and are relegated to a secondary position in society. Carter argued that religion still has a strong hold on people's minds, especially those of the poor and uneducated masses, who are looking to the holy texts for guidance in coping with the world today, and that it should take greater responsibility for ensuring that women's rights are respected.

Religion is integral to culture and tradition worldwide, influencing the patterns of thought and modes of behaviour of billions of people. What would happen if believers of all faiths began to listen to women imams, rabbis, monks and priests preaching and praying? They would definitely grow to respect women more, and not just in a religious context.

Women and religion
The Bible, like all other sacred texts, was written by men; men who portrayed God as being male. Why? It was Pope Luciani who said, 'God is our father; even more he is our mother!'

The Reverend Emma Percy, a member of the WATCH council (Women and the Church), made God's gender her special focus. She argues that describing God as a 'he' in hymns and prayers makes men appear 'more god-like than women'. Emma was educated at Oxford and embraced the feminist movement long ago. Since the beginning of the 1980s, she has been writing about feminism, Christianity and the role of the woman within the Anglican tradition: 'When we use only male language for God, we reinforce the idea that God is like a man,' she points out. According to Emma Percy, the Bible uses *feminine* imagery. She argues that gender is part of the human dimension; God is above all this. If we talk about God as a man, it is just because it has become a tradition and traditions have always been carried on by men. If we were clear on this point, a second Copernican revolution could begin. The female gender would regain universal dignity and respect, even in the religious sphere.

God's gender assumes greater importance in contexts where femininity is an integral part of religious belief, as in India. In India there are puzzling contradictions in terms of women's emancipation: on the one hand, there is unparalleled violence and constant discrimination towards women, especially among the poorest classes. But on the other, women rise to become strong and powerful political leaders. How is this possible?

Religion plays a key role in shaping social imagery. Hindu theology contains a very strong ideal of the goddess, a sort of great protecting mother. That is why a succession of women have followed one another into high political office: Indira Gandhi, Mayawati, Pratibha Patil, Mamata Banerjee. Nevertheless, motherhood is the role they are intended for; they are raised as mothers of the country, mothers of sons, and mothers are oppressed and dismissed as worthless if they do not give birth.

British rule did much to relieve the Indian woman's plight, abolishing such barbaric customs as *suttee* – the self-immolation of widows on their husbands' funeral pyres – at the beginning of the nineteenth century. After their husband's death, a widow was no longer worth anything and their life became meaningless. Suicide was their only option. *Suttee* was a symbol of extreme submission. The reform that abolished it – together with the 1856 act that recognised the right of widows to remarry and the Sarda Act of 1929 that forbade marriage for girls under fourteen years of age – was a major watershed in terms of the Indian woman's condition. Before the Sarda Act, girls were forced into marriage when they were extremely young and frequently became widows very soon after, entering a limbo of exclusion and poverty. A painful and humiliating virtual death in the eyes of society.

Once they had gained their right to life, Indian women had to fight to win their right to education, their first real weapon against exclusion. The part played in this struggle by Hindu activists was crucial. Among them was Pandita Ramabai, daughter of a Brahmin who defied nineteenth-century convention to give his child a Sanskrit education. This enlightened man was deeply convinced that depriving women of education amounted to tyranny. It was not even justified by the Hindu holy texts. Thanks to him, to his wisdom and his love, millions of girls gained their right to education. This is an example of how the joint action of men and women, in this case father and daughter, can play a key role in the assertion of civil rights. When her husband died, Pandita Ramabai suffered the Indian widow's usual loss of status. She converted to Anglicanism and became an activist for women's rights.

In patriarchal cultures, such as the Jewish and earlier Christian ones, husbands own their wives; a wife's role is virtually that of an obedient, child-bearing domestic drudge. Obviously, these cultures were created to suit men. Even today, although the patriarchal social construct has been discredited, many men struggle to abandon such a model, and it is still one passively accepted by numerous women.

Polygamy was adopted by many patriarchal societies. If we turn to the Bible, we learn that King Solomon had seven hundred wives and three hundred concubines! Polygamy lasted beyond biblical times in the Jewish world, though few men could afford such a luxury. It was declared illegal in the eleventh century, but women continued to be kept in subjugation.

Even today, within Judaism only men can hold religious office. The film *Yentl* exposes this injustice with insight and deep sensitivity. The young protagonist is a rabbi's daughter who grows up studying the Talmud and the Torah. When she is left an orphan, social convention requires her to marry a devout Jew, but the young Yentl has other ideas. She is interested in taking up rabbinic studies, something which, as a woman, she is forbidden to do. She decides to dress up as a man and enter a yeshiva, a religious Jewish school. There she encounters love and has, again, to choose between her freedom and observing social conventions.

Within the Catholic Church the figure of the priest is still invariably male. Women can choose a religious life as a nun but they cannot celebrate Mass. However, the history of Christianity is rich in female figures. Among them, Ildegarda di Bingen was well known for her contribution to theology, medicine and the arts, especially music and poetry. Saint Ildegarda used to encourage her sisters to live each day with joy and gratitude, in harmony with the universe. Accounts of life in the monastery she founded on the River Rhine speak of beautiful female voices singing Gregorian chants, nuns adorned with flowers during religious feasts, refuge and medical treatment provided for any girl who knocked at the door of the convent. Saint Ildegarda used her feminine qualities to enhance her faith, and approached everything she did from a highly original perspective. Pope Francis himself stresses the importance of feminine spirituality. He refutes widely held superstitions about temptresses. He argues that there is room for the theology of any woman who is worthy of God's blessing.

Women's condition within Islam is definitely not something to be celebrated. Many Muslim women still endure the sort of treatment their Western sisters got rid of in the twentieth century. Islam has been misrepresented and exploited by men, and has been used to legitimise tyranny and violence of every kind. In countries like Afghanistan and Iran, women do not have the right to take part in social activities or public events and they risk detention and corporal punishment if they do not wear a headscarf or cover their bodies with all-enveloping robes. Moreover, they have limited access to public places. Men and women do not associate outside the home; a rigid policy of segregation which allows young fundamentalists to gain the maximum control over the female population.

A life hedged about with such restrictions is hard to imagine for Western women. In 1984, Betty Mahmoody, a young American woman married to an Iranian doctor, had a painful first-hand experience of what it can mean. That year, Betty and her husband Sayed left for a short trip to visit his parents in the Iranian capital. With them was their five-year-old daughter Mahtob. After a few days, Sayed told his wife that he wanted to settle in Teheran. Betty didn't want that: in Iran, she knew, life for women was difficult; she feared for her daughter and for herself. Sayed, backed by his family, kept her confined to the home against her will, forced Mahtob to attend the Islamic school, made both of them wear headscarves and monitored all their movements. The lack of an American embassy in Teheran made things even worse, although, since she was married to an Iranian man, her American citizenship had no value there anyway. Moreover, Islamic law provides that, in the event of divorce, a mother loses all rights of access to her children. Betty had to make a choice: either to split up with Sayed and abandon Mahtob or to risk her life by running away with her daughter. With a local woman's help, Betty and Mahtob set out on the long and perilous journey to Turkey. Once across the border, they managed finally to reach the American embassy in Ankara safe and sound. Today Betty Mahmoody runs One World, an association committed to protecting the universal rights of mothers and children in countries where those rights are not recognised.

In Mauritania, an Islamic republic where the division of society into castes still survives and a country where there are more slaves than in any other, Mohamed Ould Mkhaitir was sentenced to death for apostasy just because he wrote on a social network that Islam has backed social inequality since the time of Mohammed and that it was the responsibility of politics – not of religion – to put an end to it. Mohamed was held in solitary confinement in a two-metre cell. Even the other prisoners wanted to kill him for his declaration. Upon his arrest no lawyer had the courage to defend him. The only voice raised in his support was that of a woman; a feminist called Aminetou Mint El-Moctar. This heroine is the president of an organisation that has had to banish all reference to human rights from its name and as a result is called l'Association des Femmes Chefs de Famille (AFCF) – Women who are Head of the Household. Aminetou Mint El-Moctar is an inspiration; she is brave, she is modern. But she is alone.

Aminetou really is one of a kind. She herself experienced the horror of a forced marriage when she was still a young girl of thirteen but, instead of being broken by this, she started fighting for women's rights. Because of her fight against the reigning patriarchy in Mauritania, she was arbitrarily arrested and detained on several occasions. She has regularly been scorned and stigmatised and has had to cope with intimidation aimed at her family and members of the association she runs. She has even been subjected to death threats. In 2014, she was the object of a fatwa (a religious death sentence issued by a senior Muslim dignitary) for her defence of Mohamed Mkhaitir. She went into exile for several months and, upon her return in 2015, her son was also threatened with death and she was forced to send him abroad in order to protect him. Her life, the life of a rebel who constantly stands up for the rights of women, of minorities and of all those deprived of their civil liberties, should be an example for everyone.

To deprive the enemy of dignity is the oppressor's first move. Just think about the Nazis' persecution of the Jews, the American colonists' treatment of black slaves, or, simply, what is still happening today to many women in the world. But the tragic truth is that women themselves carry on the traditions and rituals that oppress them. The explanation of this phenomenon lies in the inadequacy of education. Knowledge is power. Without real knowledge, fear and superstition will be handed down by mothers to their daughters in a chain of suffering that is impossible to break. If we do not intervene radically to reform male culture and female education we will never evolve.

In a world ravaged by fanaticism, the future depends on women. They need to take their bodies, their identity and their dignity back. They need to educate the men of the future and banish violence from the centuries to come. They need to teach their children the meaning of *love* and compassion for all human beings. However long the battle lasts, we will win in the end. Maybe women need a new religion, a revised gospel to remind them how precious and lovable they are. Meanwhile, we can just ask men the question Olympe de Gouges posed in her *Declaration of the Rights of Woman and of the Female Citizen*: 'Man, are you capable of being fair? A woman is asking.'

3
Work is Freedom

'We have to free half of the human race, the
women, so that they can help to free the other half.'

Emmeline Pankhurst

Work and emancipation

Women have been oppressed by the institutions of
religion and marriage ever since their inception and have
suffered centuries of subservience under their hegemony.
Today women have the right – and the duty – to free
themselves from a culture that would still, if it could, keep
them dependent, subjugated and unhappy. Emancipation
means freedom from restraint, and to be truly emancipated
we need to take control of our own lives.

Women *really* gain that control through work. What
is guaranteed on paper can materialise thanks to work.
Wherever women's rights are acknowledged, economic
self-sufficiency creates the necessary conditions for social
upgrading. Only the right to work grants equality and
dignity to women.

Nowadays, for many of us a career is fundamental to
our life. Economic self-sufficiency has become a priority.
Let us take an example of how things have changed. In
his book *The Fashion System*, semiotician Roland Barthes
revisited the symbolic meaning of jewellery. Highly
precious and typically feminine accessories were created
for women as outward signs of their husbands' wealth:
they were a repository of male power. But jewellery has

changed its meaning today: a working woman can wear jewellery she has bought with her own money. She has ceased to be a mere exhibitor of male success and has become the image of *her own* fulfilment.

However, although women have been excluded from the world of work for centuries, many of them have nonetheless become commercial icons, creating economic empires basically out of nowhere. One such icon is Madame Clicquot. A widow at the age of twenty-seven, she took control of the small wine shop that belonged to her husband. The wines of Clicquot's shop started to be exported all over the world, increasing in fame and quality. In 1814, the widow even challenged the continental barriers that had long paralysed European trade by transporting her wines for sale in Saint Petersburg. The popularity of her wine cellar rose exponentially thanks to the *veuve*'s intuition, initiative and passion. She used to personally check her merchandise at every stage of its journey, from production to distribution. Today Veuve Clicquot champagne is a luxury product, well known throughout the world for its quality and distinction.

Another woman who became a legend thanks to her exceptional abilities is Coco Chanel. Daughter of a peddler, she grew up in an orphanage run by the Congregation of the Sacred Heart. At eighteen, she moved to Moulins where she worked as a seamstress and a singer in some *concert-cafés*. In those years she started sewing hats and nine years after leaving the Sacred Heart she opened her first boutique on the rue Cambon in Paris. When her customers – initially middle-class women – began to commission dresses, Chanel's style stood out in all its newness; in an age when women were still prisoners of corsets, long dresses and showy accessories, the young fashion designer made simplicity the essence of her brand. She got rid of corsets, shortened dresses and reduced the trimmings and decoration on hats and bags. Stealing ideas from men's collections, she created a new female prototype, free in her movements and refined in her sleek lines. Her models used to have short hair and a tanned complexion, symbols of a practical and active female lifestyle: women were no longer ornaments of domestic life. Coco Chanel built up a fashion empire consisting today of more than two hundred boutiques. From *concert-cafés* to catwalks, her new woman, lively and emancipated, has conquered the world.

Examples such as the widow Clicquot and Coco Chanel do not only belong to the past. One of the major literary figures of recent years, for instance, is Joanne Rowling, the creator of the most popular wizard of all time. Harry Potter's whole saga was conceived during a very tough period of her life. After having been through a divorce and lost her job, she was beset by financial problems and facing the prospect of raising her daughter on state benefits only. According to Joanne, writing was the only way to escape the crisis she was facing. In the evenings spent at her brother-in-law's pub, the character of Harry Potter took shape, together with the plots of his adventures. In 1997, a renowned publishing house, Bloomsbury, offered to publish the manuscript but asked her to assume a male pseudonym. The publisher feared that the target audience of young teenagers would not be drawn to a female writer. For that reason, Joanne suggested they use her initials and surname only: J.K. Rowling. But she did not need to hide for long: the success of her novels was overwhelming. Harry Potter became a leading brand.

Films, gadgets, theme parks; Joanne Rowling gave birth to a magical world, able to seduce young and old alike. In 2003, the American magazine *Forbes* listed her as being one of the richest women in the United Kingdom.

The importance of women's employment should not be underestimated by Western democracies (among which Italy is lagging behind in terms of its job market) or by developing countries. Many people joined the debate when Auxilia Ponga, from UN Women, argued that gender equality should be at the core of each developing enterprise, including those concerned with finance. Without equality no sustainable growth is possible.

Nobel Peace Prize winner Muhammad Yunus, well known for his Grameen Bank – a bank providing loans to the poorest without any security – underlined the need to put our faith in women for the growth of a country. They are more sensible and willing to accept sacrifices, he said, especially in the developing countries. Yunus focused on women customers entirely, providing them with micro-credits through the good offices of his bank. He contributed to women's emancipation in countries that need it most, such as Bangladesh and India, and not only did he bring economic progress, but also social welfare. This is why Yunus was awarded the Nobel Peace Prize instead of the Nobel Prize for Economics, as expanded upon in the committee's citation: 'Lasting peace cannot be achieved unless large population groups find ways to break out of poverty.'

Women's emancipation breaks the cycle of marginalisation. In Arab countries – as in some Western societies, such as the small towns of Southern Italy – women do not have any opportunities. Their value resides in their role as wives and mothers. Why is it that women, who are equal to men in terms of intelligence, creative spirit and will, have been denied the possibility of economic emancipation? During the first centuries AD, many women were persecuted not only for religious reasons but also because they refused to marry a man chosen for them by their family. Even a life dedicated to meaningful study was out of the question. Men always ruled over wives, daughters and sisters.

Increasing women's employment in a country suffering from unemployment means not only contributing to its development but also fighting against domestic abuse. When a woman has a job, she gains more dignity in the eyes of her partner, she feels independent, has high self-esteem and does not tolerate either physical or psychological violence. She is not afraid of leaving a man who beats and humiliates her since she knows she can manage without him.

Requirements for women to achieve economic self-sufficiency

In order to help more women successfully enter the job market, it is essential to provide them with education and to increase their visibility. Education is the gateway to employment: without it, no rewarding job can be found. In previous centuries, women could not access education and therefore work was denied them. Only after having reached economic self-sufficiency can women aim at a healthy social role, a *wholeness* of domestic and professional fulfilment. Therefore, the order of change must be: education, work, independence, fulfilment.

Nobel Peace Prize winner Malala Yousafzai has fought for girls' right to education for a long time and has risked her life in the process: when she was only fourteen years old, she was hit in the head by a bullet while taking the bus to school. Malala had been a Taliban target for three years following an informative blog she wrote for the BBC on their regime in Pakistan. She became an icon in the fight for girls' right to education and delivered a speech at the UN, in which she said, 'So let us wage a glorious struggle against illiteracy, poverty and terrorism, let us pick up our books and our pens, they are our most powerful weapons. One child, one teacher, one book and one pen can change the world. Education is the only solution. Education first.'

Visibility and audibility are other important requirements for women's emancipation. These are far from being marginal issues: it is fundamental to let women's voices be raised and listened to. When situations offer opportunities, women must be quick to seize them. Every day, in Italy and around the world, a wide variety of conventions are being held. They may be conferences on medicine, law, social politics, climate change or technological progress. Speakers are called to talk onstage with a microphone and a light pointed straight at them. Their names appear on fliers or on social networks. They gain popularity and authority. According to research carried out by the think tank PariMerito, there is a marked difference between panels of speakers in Italy and panels in other Western countries like the USA and the UK; it seems in my country, very few women are asked to speak at conferences. Holding a conference allows those who are less known to be listened to and appraised, not only during the event itself, but even after, when there are social gatherings or opportunities to network with journalists and other professionals. Relationships established on a professional level are extremely important. In more than 90 per cent of cases, such conventions feature a majority of male speakers. Sometimes, there are just one or two women out of six or more speakers. Every time we ask the conference organisers why, they all react in the same way: at first, they get flustered; they do not understand why excluding women from the panel may be a problem. After it has been explained to them that diversity is an indispensable value within society and that it is necessary to give visibility to female talents as well, the organisers apologise, while making a variety of excuses:

- they do not know where to find female speakers
- their chosen female speakers were busy
- there were no available women for the roles required at the conference

Diversity should be a *sine qua non*. The importance of women's participation at conferences and seminars cannot be overestimated. The researchers at PariMerito aim to continue monitoring the number of female speakers at conferences and seminars carried out in Italy and intervening when the number falls below 15 per cent. Men are still reluctant to offer visibility and authority to women. My native country – and, unfortunately, many others too – is not meritocratic. We have women managers, businesswomen and female scientists but nobody knows who they are. We do not only fight for diversity; we want to promote an ethical code consisting of three requirements:

- visibility for women
- high-standard networking
- female role models for the public

It is vital to have female role models in order to convince others that women are capable of expressing their opinions on a stage; that they can be listened to and taken seriously. Visibility is strictly connected to electoral success. If the public are not exposed to authoritative and capable women, they will not vote for other female candidates since they are conditioned to believe that only men can be leaders.

If we analyse regional elections in Italy in places where there are candidates of both genders, a discouraging fact emerges: even women do not vote for other women. In 2015's regional elections in Puglia, the top five candidates for the Democratic Party were all female and none were elected.

In fact, the most popular medium, television, is the main influence on political elections. On political talk shows, the usual disproportion can be found with every channel: the: speakers are mostly men. The producers of the programmes call expert politicians and well-known intellectuals, but no women are high-profile enough to be invited. PariMerito investigated such talk shows and found that in only one of the 145 broadcast episodes they studied was there an acceptable ratio of male to female guests:

- *Ballarò*: January-November 2015 (33 episodes), 311 guests, 76 women only = 24.4%
- *Che tempo che fa* and *Che fuori tempo che fa*: January-June 2015 (42 episodes), 208 guests, 25 women only = 12%

- *Porta a Porta*: January-May 2015 (70 episodes), 666 guests, 180 women only = 27%

These depressing results portray a country where women have few opportunities and therefore less visibility, and vice versa – a real catch-22 situation with no way out. And these revelations are even more shameful when we remember that they relate to programmes put out by Rai, a public-service provider. Depriving viewers of worthy female role models to get inspired by is a disservice. That is why a new regulation within the company would be desirable, compelling balanced gender representation in its several talk shows. Talking about gender quotas has always been a slippery slope, but our proposal for an internal regulation within Rai arises from awareness: for each male businessman, lawyer, journalist, politician, engineer, doctor or 'expert' in some field, there will be a woman similarly qualified. The aim is not to force somebody's hand to create an artificial equality, but to make the editorial staff represent the real country. Getting out of this rut and filling TV with a variety of voices can give rise to livelier discussion, to new ideas and an innovative image.

A woman candidate in an election is less likely to be elected if she has been deprived of a platform from which to put forth her policies. It goes without saying that issues linked with femininity, such as maternity or equal opportunities, are disregarded by a political establishment made up of men only. This being the case, women's journey towards self-determination continues to be difficult.

In Italy, as well as in many other countries all over the world, we are preventing more than half the population from expressing itself and changing the country for the better. But also we are depriving ourselves of a wealth of talent that could enrich our system. A major shift in dynamics should be our priority.

Female employment worldwide

Nowadays, women have gained their right to work in most parts of the world. Paradoxically, in Western countries, women moved from the home into the workplace out of necessity when, during World War I, the men were away fighting in the trenches. In countries like Saudi Arabia, where women were not even allowed to drive until 2018, there has been no equivalent change in their circumstances. Technology and science have developed, but women's rights have not. There are even countries where political leaders try to reverse any progress made in the past!

Just look at the case of Turkey. In the 1920s, Turkish leader Kemal Atatürk granted full social and political rights to women. He turned the Turkish Islamic State into a secular country and his top priority was women's emancipation. He banished polygamy, changed succession rights, validated female testimony in court and improved education. He allowed women to work, and abolished compulsory headscarves. Erdogan, the current Turkish president, in contrast, has reintroduced headscarves in schools. In November 2014 he made a bewildering declaration saying that women can aspire only to be mothers, a declaration that threatens to turn back the clock on progress! Unfortunately, with few women in politics and a high percentage of female unemployment, there is a risk that Prime Minister Erdogan will succeed in his effort to drive women back into the home, thus reinstating old discriminatory practices.

Female employment is the measure of a thriving society. When it is too low, it affects younger generations as well. Turkey is not as behind as we may think. The female employment rate of some regions in Southern Italy is, at 31 per cent, equal to Turkey's. In this respect, the most enviable countries are the Northern European democracies: Sweden, the Netherlands, Norway and Denmark. In these countries, female employment is equal to male employment – just as it should be in a healthy economy.

The contribution of women is fundamental. Angela Merkel, chancellor of one of the most high-functioning countries in terms of equal opportunities, argues that working women are a resource that greatly boosts GNP, a resource to be consolidated through financial assistance and improved conditions. If female employment is high, the whole country will benefit from better welfare provision. In addition, the birthrate will constantly grow once women know they can count on state support during maternity leave.

In Northern Europe, the glass ceiling keeping women out of politics is a thing of the past. Former Prime Minister of Denmark Helle Thorning-Schmidt is proof of that. In Sweden, 43 per cent of the Parliament is made up of women. These are countries with a high standard of living and the services offered by the government are many, especially as far as family welfare is concerned. Again, Angela Merkel has described the situation precisely, arguing that the countries where women lead and participate in economic, political and public life tend to be more inclusive and democratic, and enjoy a higher level of economic development.

The European strategy to increase female employment is called flexicurity; it provides job-market flexibility, granting employment assurance at each life stage. Flexicurity provides women with a place in society. It lets them fulfil themselves in terms of work, according to their ambitions and capabilities, and establish social relationships outside of their family. Couples with a double income run a lower risk of poverty and have more resources in the event of crisis situations. That is why it is important to grant flexicurity. It is one of the most revolutionary legacies of the twentieth century.

Let us look at the USA. In the United States the political and social systems are meritocratic. Ex-President Barack Obama acknowledged this, and singled out communities offering equal opportunities to women as being the most peaceful, prosperous and best educated. In the USA, public opinion is generally more favourable to the cause of women and aware that a more equal representation of gender is important. Newspapers and TV often host successful women, role models to girls and boys; the adults to be. In contrast, for centuries Italy's daughters have not had female role models to get inspired by. It is time for all this to change.

Unfortunately, even in the most state-of-the-art democracies, many women are compelled to choose between having a career or a family. In the USA, 49 per cent of women in high-level positions do not have children. Among men, only 19 per cent are childless. Women's professional fulfilment can come at too high a cost. Real emancipation should not involve such a sacrifice.

Today, women are still paid less than men to carry out the same tasks with equal responsibilities. That is truly unfair. In Italy, such a phenomenon is scarcely mentioned, but abroad equal pay is a highly valued issue. Italian women can be paid as much as 30 per cent less than their male colleagues. Why? On the one hand they do not negotiate job offers themselves. On the other, businessmen offer women a lower salary.

A high rate of female employment is not always a guarantee of emancipation. Let us consider Asia. In countries like China, female employment is extremely high, but most of the work is hard, physical toil, such as agricultural labouring. The percentage drops dramatically when it comes to more powerful jobs providing economic security. Agricultural work is uncertain and does not allow for advancement, whilst providing for primary needs only. In other words, it keeps women in a condition of permanent reliance. It is false emancipation.

Women and technology

Very few women choose to study science, technology, engineering or maths. This is regrettable because, currently, the most interesting and best-paid jobs are to be found in these disciplines. Technology is the future; women cannot disregard this, girls must not neglect these fields of study. Society conveys the message: 'Science is a matter for men.' The culture we are rooted in influences us more than our parents do.

We need to take steps to interest girls in scientific and technological subjects. We need to provide them with valuable role models. Children identify with what surrounds them. Everything matters: nursery-school teaching, fairy tales told by mothers, the words of parents, teachers and educators. In one of her first interviews,

Randi Zuckerberg — sister of the well-known Mark who created the social network we know as Facebook — said, 'My brother got video games, I got dolls.' Luckily, the role models girls do have in science and technology are impressive ones.

In November 2014, Samantha Cristoforetti, a young Italian astronaut, left for the International Space Station where she spent two hundred days — a record among European astronauts. After her engineering studies at Air University and further training courses in the USA, Samantha was chosen from among 8,500 candidates. Her stay in space was closely followed by the whole of Italy.

History is rich in examples of women who have excelled in science but, as usual, only a few of them received the recognition they deserved. Jocelyn Bell, a British astrophysicist, had to contend with male chauvinism in academia to have her work acknowledged. During her PhD studies in Cambridge, under Professor Antony Hewish, Jocelyn discovered a new source of energy in space, a neutron star that moves at high speed releasing regular pulsations: the pulsar. Her discovery won the Nobel Prize in Physics, only it was her professor who was honoured with the title. Currently, Jocelyn Bell is considered one of the major astrophysicists in the world.

In Europe, only nine software developers out of every hundred are women. In the USA, just 2 per cent of women graduate in information technology. In Silicon Valley the female employment rate is very low. Managers justify themselves by saying it is not their fault if girls do not choose the right course of study at university. It is another catch-22 situation: a culture that does not stimulate girls' curiosity towards scientific subjects makes sure a woman cannot find work in these fields, turning such studies into an exclusively male preserve.

The pressure of public opinion in the United States is so great that the giants of Silicon Valley such as Google, eBay and Twitter are forced to publish 'diversity reports'; annual reports disclosing the ratio of men to women in the workforce. The latest report reveals that out of every eight employees in technical roles, only one is a woman.

Not only must we fight against discrimination, but we must think too about the future. As the former European Commissioner for the Digital Agenda, Neelie Kroes, has impressed upon women, 'Technology is too important to be left to men.'

So why was the participation of more than a hundred women at the IT marathon in Bangalore, South India, somehow not considered news. Despite there being an all-female 'hackathon'. Despite those women working for three consecutive days at open-source humanitarian projects – that is to say on free-of-charge software. Even despite the event being part of the fourth worldwide computing conference organised by The Grace Hopper Celebration of Women in Computing and by Systers, the major virtual community of women experts in computers, counting more than three thousand female members in fifty-four countries around the world. It is not considered news, but it is news.

Let us take a step back. The IT marathon has educational and social purposes. It represents an opportunity to contribute to the development of humanitarian projects with the help of volunteers, experts in the field. IT's greatest minds attend it – many of them women – and they all meet in India. Both the branch of study and the country in which it took place are areas where women fight hard to reach equality. The hundred women of the 'hackathon' worked on three projects:

- the creation of an 'open' technological platform to provide the poor with financial services, with the aim of helping at least two and a half billion people
- the drawing of detailed maps to ensure greater security for women, especially those who often travel to work
- the setting up of a website that will provide the poorest countries with information on drugs, vaccinations and medical examinations

What is the driving force behind such a great event? The driving force is the desire for change: professionals in the field do not want to conform to a *male* view of life. Anita Borg explained it well. She was the founder of the Institute for Women in Technology, today called the Anita Borg Institute, and of Systers – both strictly female associations – and has been criticised for her choices, which were labelled 'discriminatory' in some quarters. Anita is unrepentant and explained that every day women have to work almost exclusively with male colleagues, with no possibility of enjoying an element of female company – a situation common within the world of work. For that gender imbalance to be redressed, it is necessary for women to talk to each other, share female role models whose example can improve their self-esteem and critical thinking. Systers was founded to promote such interaction, and it works.

During the 2015 Expo in Milan, the Women for Expo Association, headed by Emma Bonino, brought an important consideration to the public's attention: that the issue of world hunger and food waste caused by the inefficient distribution of global resources might at last find a turning point under the direction of women. Women represent 40 per cent of the agricultural workforce on the earth. Besides, they are responsible for nourishment in all cultures. With their contribution at a higher level, food production would increase considerably and waste would be limited in developed countries. Women must access technology, financing and education: today, agriculture is strictly linked with these three factors. Once engaged, women could save the world not only from war but also from the plague of hunger.

Women need to gather and nurture a uniquely feminine feeling of cohesion. Nowadays, in the developed world we have all we need: knowledge, information, technology, skills, money. But we lack a meaningful way of uniting all these elements. We have knowledge, but we lack understanding. We have resources but we lack the awareness to use them for the common good. We lack 'heart intelligence'. What can we do? Jodi Forlizzi, Director of the Human-Computer Interaction Institute at Carnegie Mellon University in Pittsburgh, encourages women never to forget what they know they are: *sensitive*. A word meaning 'in touch with one's own inner guide, responsive to one's intimate nature'.

When we allow ourselves to be ourselves we help the world most. And that is saying a lot.

Female employment in Italy

Female employment in Italy is the lowest in Europe after Greece, a country on the verge of bankruptcy. We know that the employment rate reflects the economic stability of a whole country. In the case of Italy, the female employment rate differs dramatically between North and South. In the South, the employment rate is 35.6 per cent. In the North it rises up to 56.1 per cent. The exclusion of women from the world of work in Southern Italy is so serious that we have to label the phenomenon the 'Southern Women's Issue'.

This disparity in the female employment data makes Italy sound like two different countries: the North, more like Europe, and the South, nearer to Turkey and Africa. The fact that Southern economic backwardness goes hand in hand with serious gender inequality is an extension of this analogy. During the Lisbon Council in 2000, the EU countries agreed a target of 60 per cent employment by 2010 among women between 15 and 64 years old. In 2014, in contrast to the 64 per cent overall European female employment rate among 35- to 64-year-olds, the South of Italy was still stuck at 35.6 per cent. Among less-educated women, only 28.3 per cent were employed. The total employment rate in Italy was 47.8 per cent. Shall we become a country where women have given up on economic self-sufficiency?

Such economic backwardness has to be looked at in its cultural context. I am often stunned when I listen to what Southern Italian women say. Many of them, unconsciously, are fulfilled only thanks to the man they married. They are so absorbed by the idea that marriage is the first and most important way of fulfilment that they judge other women on this basis. Just men matter: they *complete* women. Without a partner a woman is only a half.

You often hear people saying, 'How can such a wonderful woman be single?!' Behind this question lies a lot of prejudice. First of all, the speaker is usually judging a woman only on the basis of her physical appearance, without taking into account her intelligence and skills. Secondly, they think that a relationship is the key to success every woman should aim for. It is precisely due to this thinking that an unmarried woman was not so long ago called 'Miss' until she was ninety. A man, on the other hand, was addressed as a 'young gentleman' until eighteen, and then he was called 'Mr' because he was considered adult even without a wife.

The issue becomes crucial when a woman has to choose between finding her fulfilment in her studies and job or looking for a man to marry so that he can support her. The latter choice often turns out badly when times of social change frequently bring divorce and unemployment. An employed woman who devotes herself to her career chooses a modern and emancipated lifestyle, and if she marries, her husband plays an active, modern role within the family.

The 'working society' confers upon its members, both men and women, social identity, independence and self-esteem. In contrast are the lives of solitude and discomfort that millions of housewives experience every day, when they get older and their children have grown up: they are bored, have no social role, no possibility of intellectual growth. They feel they have no value. They often lose respect for the man, who many years before had promised them undying loyalty, and they end up alone. Inequality within the female job market in Italy becomes more starkly evident when we compare variations of region and education as well as age. Remuneration of the national wage shifts between a maximum of 80-90 per cent for women graduates and a minimum of 12-20 per cent for less educated women. So, the South of Italy can be saved by its women via increased identity awareness, greater access to higher education and mass entry into the job market. Their children will then learn from their mothers' experience. After all, several studies show that the daughters and sons of women fulfilled in their jobs become independent, dynamic and respectful adults.

Since in Southern Italy the considerable risk of 'permanent underdevelopment' persists – one person in three still lives in a family whose income is below 60 per cent of the average salary – it is necessary to redress the regional imbalance, to provide higher incentives to employers who offer jobs to women. Another discouraging fact is the degree to which women's employment is undervalued. In the 18 to 29 age group, women's employment rate is 35.4 per cent in comparison to 48.4 per cent for their male peers. Moreover, women are paid less. Among employees, the average annual gross salary is €27,228 for women but €30,676 for men, meaning that women earn 11.2 per cent less. The condition of women graduates is even more difficult: 52 per cent of employed women are overqualified compared to 41.7 per cent of employed men. This also explains the widespread discouragement of Italian women who have given up looking for a job: women's inactivity rate is 48.9 per cent but in the rest of Europe, it does not rise above 35.5 per cent. Basically, we are dropping entire generations of women because of cultural prejudices and the effective failure to adopt policies which would invest in their future. All considered, the low growth of the country is not surprising. This is not a country for women. But it could become one, if only our government wanted it so.

The imbalance of the job market leads to increasing differences in terms of women's pensions, currently 40 per cent lower than men's. Such a discrepancy is even more humiliating if we think in terms of the domestic work that Italian women have always carried out. Housewives are never respected enough; they are physically worn out and always suffer the effects in old age. The European Council invited the Commission and the Member States to rectify the discrepancy, suggesting the introduction of a specific female pension scheme and of equal remuneration for men and women. These results can be obtained with the help of flexible work shifts, structures for children and elderly people, and an equal distribution of the unpaid work of caring for the house and children. These are measures to be considered as a whole which could significantly improve the lifestyle of Italian women and men. Once again, provided we want it to be so.

Once, people used to think that it was fair to confine women to the home. Luckily, we are no longer peasants and that form of patriarchal society does not exist any more. Everything has changed. In times of crisis, single-income families are exposed to thousands of unknowns and cannot afford luxuries, holidays, comfort. Women want and *have* to work. On the other hand, work discourages them from having children, since they are not sure whether they can raise them, and the resultant stress decreases their fertility. In Western economies, such as ours, the fertility and birth rates usually have a strictly positive correlation. Italian women have stopped having children as they cannot *plan* a family. And this is a problem for the whole society.

Let us imagine the future state of affairs if this pattern continues. If in forty years' time the Italian women's employment rate does not reach European levels, the country will be crowded with elderly people on low pensions resulting from the contribution-based system and men with temporary contracts or off-the-books jobs. It will be a country where the majority of women get the minimum pension. Today it amounts to €450 per month. How can they live like that?

Women's low level of employment depends on many factors and especially on cultural ones. In the South, patriarchal culture is still very strong. Women have to take care of the house. If they work they cannot carry out their duties as wives and mothers. This conviction is firmly established in the minds of many people, especially those of elderly men. It influences both women and their potential employers.

How many times have we seen women choosing not to work and then living to regret it? Perhaps they come to resent being entirely dependent on their husbands. Or maybe because they are envious when they see their girlfriends or acquaintances fulfilling themselves professionally. Unfortunately, when women regret their decision to stay at home, it is often too late: in a static job market like ours it is hard to find employment after having never worked or having been long out of the market, especially if you are no longer young.

A good mother is a working mother who sets an example to her children of sacrifice and duty. Children benefit from being raised by both parents sharing equal responsibilities.

How to increase women's employment

The problem of female employment has deep roots, but it is not unsolvable. We can intervene to change attitudes in schools and immigrant communities. Women passing through the child-rearing years should be gainfully employed in every sector of society.

Schooling

Education is fundamental to attaining professional fulfilment. Study opens up a world of opportunity. It allows us to discover our own attitudes and aspirations. Without education we are destined to be unemployed or underpaid and bound to humiliating jobs.

Can you remember hearing it said that knowledge is power? Graduates get the most interesting and best-paid jobs. The more highly qualified you are, the more job opportunities you get and the greater the salary you command. Unfortunately, that is not true in Italy. Despite 60 per cent of Italian women being graduates, the same percentage is unemployed. Why?

First, as we have seen, there are cultural reasons: many women give priority to their family and choose to marry straight after having finished their studies. They do not spend time looking for a job. Then, there is the job-market issue. Employers are often reluctant to hire a young woman: they think she represents a non-refundable investment in that she is likely to get pregnant soon after getting the job, forcing them to train and pay someone else.

Maternity

Maternity in Italy is well supported. While she is on maternity leave a woman is paid 80 per cent of her usual daily salary by the INPS, an institution run by the Labour Ministry. But the employer still has to pay the remaining 20 per cent, and the standard 'thirteenth salary' (a ubiquitous additional monthly salary, introduced as a result of Italy's heavy taxation), as well as finding, training and paying a substitute. This is the reason why employers prefer hiring men.

Yet we are living in the computer age, the state-of-the-art tablet age, the smart-phone age. Why not allow pregnant women to work from home – depending on their health status – and not deprive society of their contribution?

In this respect, I can give you an example of something I experienced first-hand. One of my former employees, an Australian woman, Chontelle, became pregnant with her second child a few years ago. We were both really happy about it. Chontelle was so good that I hired her on a permanent contract even after knowing she was pregnant. But none of us were aware of how the maternity-leave regulations work in Italy. Chontelle wanted to keep working from home. She had a computer with a powerful processor and a telephone contract providing unlimited foreign calls. She had everything she needed in order to contact her customers without getting tired. Obviously, I was happy, too, not to lose her: she was one of the most valuable employees I had.

Everything sounded perfect. We were happy we had found a solution. Until the employment consultant phoned. Once I mentioned my employee's pregnancy, a dead silence fell. The consultant then shouted down the phone, calling us crazy. Chontelle's pregnancy was far advanced. She had to provide her maternity certificate immediately and cease any kind of work. Why? Because that was the law. I tried to explain that my employee was happy to work while she was pregnant and that she had also received bonuses related to her productivity. The consultant insisted that I had to force my employee not to work any more, nor even allow her to make calls or send e-mails. Chontelle was shocked. She could not believe it: in her country, maternity leave worked in a completely different way! I had to explain to her that this was the law in Italy and that we had to accept it.

The three-month absence of the most expert consultant on our staff led to a decrease in profits. Chontelle could not be easily replaced in the short term: training a professional like her takes years.

Maternity protection has been a big step forward for women and it absolutely should not be questioned. However, some kind of flexibility for female workers – both during their ordinary work and during maternity leave – would grant them more peace of mind. A woman would not see herself replaced by a substitute and employers would have fewer reservations about hiring her, since they would know they could count on her even during maternity leave, should she become pregnant.

Migration flows

We cannot speak about employment without taking into account the ever-increasing flow of non-EU migrants into Italy. Immigrants are an integral part of our society and we have to consider their impact on all areas of our social and working lives.

Let us look at the National Institute for Social Security (the INPS). Nowadays pensions are paid by young workers. Who will bear the cost of the ageing population in forty years' time? Immigrants themselves. Thanks to them the country will be able to count on fresh forces to compensate for its unbalanced population.

However, let us be clear that a considerable percentage of immigrants come from countries where women do not yet have equal rights and dignity. Therefore, it is up to us to change their perspective. Italy should aim to educate them: to teach a new respect and esteem for women to those who come from more socially discriminatory societies; to show them that women have a lot to offer once they are allowed to enter the world of work. This is not an easy task, and made harder by the fact that often the women in these societies are literally locked into their homes by their husbands and lack the opportunity to learn our language. They live in closed communities which don't mix with Italians. This is not a problem faced only by Italy; it is a problem common in all Western countries, including the United Kingdom. As a result of the dominant ideology of politically-correct multiculturalism, we have forgotten about women's rights and have abandoned these women to their fate as second-class citizens. This is no longer acceptable in countries that are considered equalitarian. We can't forget about these women, even if the women in question say that they are happy with this kind of life. Of course they are; they don't know any better.

It is our duty to expose both immigrant women and men to our charter of rights; to empower the former, teaching them our language and customs and to enlighten the latter by impressing on them the need to consider women not as daughters of a lesser god, but as equals deserving of freedom, respect, love and care and no violence, ever.

We should start thinking about the future, because the future is now and we have already made too many mistakes by not considering the importance of women in society. The irony inherent within multiculturalism is that, in the name of freedom and diversity, we end up enforcing the kind of inequality our liberal ethos aims to abolish. We shouldn't tolerate this anymore. Women's rights are fundamental not only for the women themselves but also for their families; for their children. These children will become the citizens of the future and we must ask ourselves what kind of citizens we want? Citizens who see their mothers constantly abused and treated as human beings of secondary importance? Citizens who think it the norm for women to lack social skills, be reclusive and devoid of independence? Citizens who accept women being treated like objects at the disposal of men, the 'guardians' of the home? We don't really want that, do we? Take notice then, because these children are already growing up and now is the time to prevent a whole new generation of women from reaching adulthood already shackled to their prescribed gender roles.

4
Born a Woman

'For all the violence imposed on her,
For all the humiliation she has suffered,
For her body that you have taken advantage of,
For her intelligence that you have walked upon,
For the ignorance in which you have left her,
For the freedom you have denied her,
For the mouth you shut,
And for the wings you clipped,
Stand Gentlemen, in front of a Woman!'

Anonymous

To be born a woman in the world

During the Boston marathon in 1967, a curious accident happened. The runners were already four miles into the race when someone shouted, 'There is a girl!' In the 1960s, women were not allowed to participate in the Boston marathon, one of the most important sporting events in America. But that day, Kathrine Switzer, a student, decided to start her own revolution. She had trained for months until she could manage 31 miles – the race is 26 miles long – and, using only her initials, she had signed up for the marathon. As soon as Jock Semple, the director of the race, saw the girl among the marathon runners, he rushed on to the track and grabbed her shoulders, trying to pull her to the side. 'Leave my race and give the bib back!' he stormed. Kathrine's boyfriend and her coach, Arnie Briggs, restrained Semple so that she could finish the race. Nobody tried to stop her again. She scored an excellent time result but her participation in the race was labelled 'unofficial'. Kathrine won the marathon some years later, in 1974. Today, she is a sports writer and a popular athlete. She achieved her ambition despite everyone and everything.

A woman confident enough to assert herself can enjoy her life as she chooses. She is fulfilled and that in itself increases her family's well-being significantly. The big problem in many African and Middle Eastern countries is that women are not free to build their own self-respect. What kind of children do subdued, undereducated, superstitious and weak women raise? What kind of men do their sons become, after seeing their mothers subjugated, humiliated, aimless and devoid of authority? The situation leads to an escalation of pain and degradation that in turn leads to wars, abuse of power and hatred.

Today, in Western democracies, many things have changed for the better. However, women still have to fight every day for their rights to be recognised and respected. By disregarding history, succeeding generations will run the risk of making worse mistakes than the preceding ones and a new male chauvinist culture may spring up. Sexism is the most deceitful and long-lasting form of discrimination. Simone de Beauvoir, a major feminist, argued that, 'Humanity is male and man defines woman not in herself but as relative to him; she is not regarded as an autonomous being.' Violence against women comes from a refusal to acknowledge women's dignity: a cultural basis legitimises this abomination. Worryingly, violence is increasing. Many men feel they have the right to beat women because they consider them to be inferior beings.

In the tragic story of the New Delhi gang rape – when six men raped a twenty-three-year-old girl on a bus, causing her to die two weeks later from her injuries – the driver argued that it had been the girl's fault, since if she had stayed at home, it would never have happened and, if she had behaved modestly, she would not have been killed. Such words make your blood run cold and say a lot about women's condition on the Indian subcontinent. It is not without reason that New Delhi has been called 'the rape capital of India'.

Yet, we do not need to go far from Western Europe to find similar crimes. For instance, the condition of women in Albania is tragic, to say the least. The *Kanun*, a code where the rules and customs of Albanian culture were listed, has left a 'poisonous' heritage which still inspires violence even though it is no longer part of the law. Article 29 actually compared women to goatskin flasks.

Today, women in Albania still live in a subordinated condition, both in cultural and legal terms: they cannot even inherit property! Domestic violence is widespread and, though the government introduced a law to punish it in 2006, a lack of subsidies for counselling to help abused women makes the law ineffective. Culture overrides the law, especially in rural and less educated areas.

In Albania, even educated women face many difficulties: they often forego degree courses to avoid moving to another city, as it is considered by family and friends to be unsuitable for a girl. If they manage to graduate, young women struggle to find a job and are forced to accept a much lower salary than men. All this is happening in a country which became an official candidate for accession into the European Union on 24 June 2014. What should the European Commission do to improve the lives of millions of Albanian women? Should not a high respect for the dignity of women be a precondition for entry into the EU?

Under the heading 'Progress on Protection of Minorities', the European Parliament website has this to report: 'The rights of women, children and vulnerable people must be secured and discrimination against lesbian, gay, bisexual and transgender (LGBT) persons and Roma combated, say MEPs, pointing to the high levels of domestic violence, forced prostitution and trafficking of women and children.' This is all very good and we hope that these noble words will lead to concrete action but why should women be included here? Women are not a minority. They represent the majority of Europe's population! There should be a special chapter solely concerning the violation of women's rights. This area of injustice should be the starting point from which all others are tackled. High levels of democratic legislation and economic growth are recorded in the countries where women's rights are recognised. In such countries, minority rights are protected as a direct consequence. When women are finally respected and treated as equals by all men all over the world, when women have equal political, economic and financial power, then minorities will be treated equally and this will be a better world for everyone.

Many Albanian women have formed a coalition to claim what is theirs by right. They have created groups such as the Independent Forum of Albanian Women, among the most active movements in Albania. Why should we not help them with their fight? Why does the EU not provide subsidies to favour the associations fighting for women's emancipation within the member states and in those countries on the waiting list to enter the EU?

In Egypt, as in many other countries, the vast majority (75 per cent) of men who use violence against women are their relatives: fathers, brothers and husbands who torture their daughters, sisters and wives for trivial reasons, for a betrayal or even for having been raped.

Female genital mutilation is another widespread form of abuse in Egypt. This practice deprives women of their clitoris, the sexual organ that imparts pleasure. The physical and mental effects are a perpetual torture. In extreme and quite common cases, the girl's vulva is entirely sutured. It will then be opened by her husband on their wedding night, causing her horrible pain. The message is clear: men can have unlimited sex but women are simply men's objects; tools for pleasure and procreation. 97 per cent of Egyptian women have suffered genital mutilation.

Selective abortion, prevalent in India and China, is a silent tragedy. It is gendercide. Pregnancy gets terminated as soon as the female sex of the baby is discovered, since having a baby girl is considered to be an economic and social burden. The female victims are not even given the right to exist. Western countries take no notice. How can they stand by and watch such an atrocity without intervening?

During the last decades of the twentieth century, we learned that the rights women have achieved over the years are not irreversible: regression is always possible, as has been the case in Turkey and Malaysia. Up to the 1970s, before the rapid spread of ultra-conservative Islam, Malaysian women could live in freedom: they used to wear showy clothes, they were happy, lively, and in harmony with the beautiful nature of their country. Unfortunately, religious prejudice took control of politics and, little by little, women lost the rights they had acquired: they started wearing headscarves, as well as dark and heavy clothes to cover themselves. These are uncomfortable clothes for a tropical country. Some Malaysian models were even arrested for having attended a beauty contest and in 2010 three twenty-year-old girls were flogged when found guilty of sexual relations outside marriage. Luckily, a feminist movement has developed in Malaysia. It tries to halt this increasing discrimination. Zainah Anwar, a well-known activist for women's rights, has fought for years with the Sisters in Islam Association (SIS) in order to reconcile the Koran's idea of justice with a more progressive model of social policy, stating that, 'It was not Islam that oppressed women, but male-centred interpretations of the Koran influenced by the cultural practices and values of a patriarchal society.'

Women in Afghanistan set an example, as well. In the 1970s, President of the Afghan Democratic Republic Nur Mohammad Taraki implemented reforms to support women's emancipation, such as those which introduced compulsory education and the right to vote. But with the advent of the Taliban, Afghan women were plunged back into the Middle Ages, an era of deprivation, violence and submission.

Islamic fundamentalism has created mechanisms by means of which faith is exploited to legitimise the sexual slavery of women and girls. Isis men, most notably, exhibit unprecedented rage: 5,000 Yazidi women – mostly girls and young women – were kidnapped, sold, passed from one owner to another, like animals. Faced with such an outrage, the world kept silent and watched. Why do the EU and UN not stand up for the rights of the victims of religious fundamentalism? We should establish a humanitarian programme aimed at saving these martyrs, taking care of and protecting those who manage to escape. The evolution of human beings is not only defined by technological and economic progress: it means the advance of civilization as a whole, including moral concerns. We should not leave these women behind. It would mean surrendering our principles. Feminist diplomacy can save the whole world.

In Western countries, feminism has ensured that women have gained full political rights and achieved economic self-sufficiency. Supporting Islamic feminist movements would be a winning strategy to improve women's conditions throughout Middle-Eastern countries. It would fit into a new worldwide diplomatic initiative in defence of women's rights. Islamic feminism is still in its infancy: the cultural context of Muslim countries is one of deep-rooted male chauvinism and our sisters certainly do not fight their war on equal terms. However, these movements can create a revolution if supported by other countries. Instead of arming guerrillas, enlightened countries should provide the women who fight to save the world with the tools to make their voices heard.

In Africa, in countries such as Nigeria where Busayo Obisakin founded WIDS (the Women Inspiration Development Center), domestic ill-treatment is the rule. There are whole villages and districts where husbands and fathers beat and torture their women, sometimes to death. None of their relatives or acquaintances blame them since this is common practice: it is always the woman's fault. They are never obedient enough. 99 per cent of these women rely on their husbands in economic terms. When and if they recover, they cannot but return to their life as slaves.

Such shameful things do not only happen in distant countries. In July 2015, a nineteen-year-old Moroccan woman, who moved to Cuneo in Italy to marry a fellow countryman, ran away from home to save herself from constant violence. He used to beat her because 'she could not cook'. The persecutor's mother was his accomplice.

In more developed countries, domestic violence is common too and not only within poor families, but also in middle and upper-middle class homes. Often, the victims themselves do not report the abuse, for the sake of their children or simply from fear. They fear they shall not be able to support themselves, that justice will not take its course and that their persecutors will take revenge. Justice is still considerably slow and mild for these kinds of crimes. How many times do we hear of women being killed by husbands or ex-partners who had already been reported? Why is domestic violence not considered a social emergency to be countered by strict rules, summary trials and structures to protect the victims? What are we waiting for to put an end to such a sick culture?

Women's bodies as property

A journey across the traditions of the world leads one to conclude that a woman's body has always been looked on as property, as something to monitor, hide or shape according to men's needs. Women are the first victims of gender discrimination. Emancipation promises women the reappropriation of their bodies. Their bodies have always been at the disposal of others, hidden, stripped of identity. Reduced to belongings or subjected to violence.

Some of the most ancient and cruel insults to women's bodies are listed below.

The corset

The corset, according to documentary evidence, was first seen in Europe in the sixteenth century. The ideal woman was an angelic creature with a tiny waist; she should move slowly, gracefully, should sigh and even lose consciousness on occasion, revealing her weakness. Though corsets conferred elegance and prettiness, they were painful and dangerous tools of mutilation: their long-term use distorted ribs and constricted the abdominal organs. They could even bring about death from internal bleeding.
WHERE IN USE: Europe, North America
WHEN IN USE: 1500-1900

The veil

In the past, the veil was worn by Catholic women to cover their hair, which was considered sexually attractive and therefore likely to lead men into temptation. In Western culture, progress has uprooted the tradition, and it remains only within female religious orders. In Islam, the veil endures. There are different kinds of veil, adopted according to the degree of social 'Islamisation'. The veil may be a hijab, a headscarf which covers the hair only; a chador, a sort of mantel which covers the woman from head to toe leaving only her face exposed; or a niqab, which leaves the eyes alone visible. To wear the veil is usually a duty, rather than a choice, but those women who do profess their freedom to choose and still continue to wear it, don't understand that real freedom is incompatible with the culture to which they submit.

WHERE IN USE: Europe, Middle East

RELIGIONS: Catholicism, Islam

WHEN IN USE: 1000 BC to the present day, but now mainly confined to Islamic countries

Foot-binding

In China, until relatively recently, a woman's role was that of total submission to men. Women were considered exploitable for centuries and a wife's only purpose was to make her husband perfectly happy.

Until the reform of the wedding law in 1950, Chinese women were considered inferior. The centuries-old practice of foot-binding ('lotus feet') is a clear example of how they were objectified. From 900 AD to the mid-twentieth century, women were victims of a barbaric custom that would permanently compromise their feet and legs, making walking difficult. From infancy girls had their feet pressed and bound, with their toes bent under their soles; a process which produced a narrowing of the heels. They would feel excruciating pain, in particular during the first two years when they ran a high risk of losing their toes through gangrene. The pain would last between two and five years. Then, women's feet would lose sensitivity and become dead appendages. Women could not work and needed their husbands' help to move. Their feet would become their partners' property. Husbands would take pleasure in stroking and massaging them. Mothers would pass the tradition on to their daughters. The sense of alienation and cultural submission experienced by women made it possible to establish this agonising torment.

WHERE IN USE: China
RELIGIONS: Taoism, Confucianism
WHEN IN USE: AD 900-1950

The burqa

The burqa came into use in Afghanistan in 1890 when the sultan wished to cover the women in his harem – his own sex slaves – so that they would not tempt other men. It is still in use within some Islamic countries, though the Koran makes no mention of it. Women wearing the burqa look like ghosts; covered by a sort of bag from head to toe, with something similar to a net over their face, they are indistinguishable from one another. They are deprived of vitamin D, due to a lack of exposure to the sun's rays, and as a consequence, they run a high risk of fractures and osteoporosis. They suffer from the heat and have difficulty walking. If a woman wearing a burqa wanted to go for a swim, she would be in danger of drowning because of the weight of the wet fabric.
WHERE IN USE: Afghanistan
RELIGION: Islam
WHEN IN USE: 1890 to the present day

Breast-ironing

This is a widespread practice in Africa. It basically involves 'ironing' girls' breasts – rubbing hot stones into them – as soon as signs of puberty appear. Again, mothers pass the torture on to their daughters, but it has nothing to do with the mother's wish to find a husband for the girl. Breast-ironing aims at hiding signs of sexual maturity, and thus reducing the risks of unwanted pregnancy and rape. It is a lack of education that gives rise to such indescribable pain. 53 per cent of girls in Cameroon are the victims

of breast-ironing. The women who suffer from it remain disabled for life; their mammary glands are permanently compromised and they run a high risk of breast cancer.
WHERE IN USE: Cameroon, Central and Western Africa
RELIGIONS: Christianity, Islam
WHEN IN USE: ancient times to the present day

Segregation or 'chaupadi'

This humiliating practice consists of separating women from the rest of the community when they are menstruating. During this time, they live in huts or in other places far from their village, since they are considered 'unclean' and dangerous. This centuries-old tradition is still widespread in Nepal and is considered acceptable by the poor, uneducated classes and the wealthy, educated ones alike. Although segregated women sometimes die of cold or starve to death, nobody will help them.
WHERE IN USE: Nepal, Middle East
RELIGIONS: Hinduism, Judaism
WHEN IN USE: ancient times to the present day

Giraffe women

These women belong to a tribe called the Karen that lives between Burma and Thailand. They are forced to wear heavy rings weighing up to ten kilogrammes in order to lengthen their necks. This practice has nothing to do with religion; it is an ancient custom. The pain starts at an early age, when the girls are between three and five years old, and it carries on throughout their whole life. Today these women are objects of curiosity for the many tourists drawn to human oddities; indeed, the UN has accused the Thai government of making money out of these victims.

WHERE IN USE: Burma and Thailand
WHEN IN USE: ancient times to the present day

'Child brides' - aka victims of legalised paedophilia

The deplorable custom of allowing men to marry young girls actually legitimises paedophilia, justifying it on a cultural basis, and victimises girls even as young as nine years old – who are of age according to Islam. Child brides get sold to ageing paedophiles who enslave them for their own brutal pleasure and demand to be waited on hand and foot. Such a tradition is still very common in India, Nigeria, Niger, Bangladesh, Ethiopia, Pakistan, Sudan, Iran, Uganda, Egypt, DR Congo, Guinea, Chad, Central African Republic, Yemen and Malawi, as well as in some parts of Turkey and Albania. In Ethiopia, 41 per cent of the female population now aged between 20 and 24 years old – that's almost two million women – were married before reaching their eighteenth birthday. And in India close to 27 million girls of this age range were child brides, with the percentage rising to as high as 65 in Rajasthan, despite the law forbidding it (UNICEF). Over 700 million women alive today were forced to marry as children and if there is no reduction in the practice, the number will reach 1.2 billion by 2050.

These numbers are calling for justice. Ending child marriage requires targeted investments from governments and international donors. Unfortunately, the funding that is currently available for long-term and structured interventions is nowhere near large enough to match the scale of child marriage worldwide. Poverty, the traditions of patriarchal societies and the low societal value of women are the primary forces that fuel early marriage.

Some Muslims who follow a conservative interpretation of sharia even argue that Islam permits child marriage. The words of Ahmad Sani Yerima, a Nigerian senator, make me shiver: 'Islamic law allows marriage not by age but by maturity, which is attained once a girl reaches the age of puberty.' These girls are treated as objects, to be given away when the family needs money. They are treated like animals, good only to make children, to provide sexual satisfaction and to clean the house. They are isolated and denied education, forced to live in a perpetual cycle of poverty.

The plight of child brides was well described by Khadija al-Salami, the first female film director in Yemen. In her documentaries, Khadija focuses on the lives of some girls who were forced to marry when they were between nine and twelve years old, and their attempts to get a divorce. The film director is the victim of a forced marriage herself. Luckily, she managed to escape. An increasingly wide distribution of her films has ensured that people in Western countries are now aware of the horror.

Even when forbidden by the law, the tradition carries on in many countries, especially in small villages. The custom has now entered Europe, brought in by immigrant communities for whom it is the norm. Countries like France, Germany and the United Kingdom are introducing preventive measures aimed at stopping the spread of the practice with the help of organisations such as the Forced Marriage Unit in London.

WHERE IN USE: India, Nigeria, Niger, Bangladesh, Ethiopia, Pakistan, Sudan, Iran, Uganda, Egypt, DR Congo, Guinea, Chad, Central African Republic, Yemen, Malawi, Turkey, Albania

RELIGIONS: Islam, Hinduism
WHEN IN USE: ancient times to the present day

Female genital mutilation

As previously discussed in relation to Egypt, infibulation, a custom of obscure and ancient origins, is the suturing of a girl's vulva that leaves holes only for the passing of urine and menstrual blood. When a woman marries, the vagina is opened to allow sexual relations – extremely painful for the bride – and to give birth. In the worst-case scenario, the procedure is followed by the removal of the clitoris, permanently depriving the victim of sexual pleasure and turning them into a mere object of male gratification. This practice was established in the Middle East and North Africa roughly 4000 years ago, but it is still common. Today it is widespread in forty countries, the majority of them Muslim. Girls subjected to infibulation suffer from severe pain all their lives and are at constant risk of infection.

In the case of genital mutilation, women again are both victims and perpetrators: grandmothers and mothers pass the tradition on to their daughters after having suffered it themselves. Within a perverse culture, an 'unsutured' woman is considered impure, non intact. She gets cast out from her social group. Infibulation guarantees a man his exclusive rights. In Ethiopia 74 per cent of women and girls between the ages of 15 and 49, equal to 23.8 million, were victims of genital mutilation as a child.
WHERE IN USE: throughout Africa and the Middle East
RELIGION: Islam
WHEN IN USE: 2000 BC to the present day

No woman is immune from the monitoring of her body, not even if she lives in one of the more developed Western countries.

Just think of the current obsession with beauty. Beauty is often seen as a key to success and social acceptance. However, society's concept of beauty is frequently artificial and achieved by means of huge sacrifices. The obsession with slim bodies, for instance, leads millions of teenagers to suffer from eating disorders, sometimes life-threatening ones. Many women undergo invasive and dangerous cosmetic surgery to achieve perfect curves, to reach the standard of beauty established by the dominant culture. Women have to be young and beautiful; wrinkles are banned in magazines, together with cellulite and skin spots. Is this not a kind of psychological violence as well? Especially for women lacking in self-esteem? Being slaves to our bodies means aiming at unattainable standards, though many of us are not aware of it.

Let us look at the fashion for stilettos. If constantly worn, they can be harmful, causing calluses, bunions, inflammation of tendons, poor stability and the potential for dangerous falls. However, fashion tells women that if they wear high heels, though uncomfortable, they will be more beautiful, more elegant and more refined than ever. Would we not be better off in a world without such conditioning, such inflated expectations? Women's freedom requires a change of attitude to beauty.

All the above-mentioned procedures spring from a common impulse: the need to master and repress women's sexuality. Women have had in the past to cover themselves and stay away from prying eyes to avoid teasing men, unless required to do so. A woman once had to be pure, stay a virgin until, when married, she became her husband's property, served him and devoted herself to his pleasure. There is no evidence of similar traditions regarding men.

Male culture has dominated women for millennia: religions, customs and traditions change but ultimately we always get to the same point. Until we face reality and act in pursuit of a radical change, we will never attain female autonomy. Allowing billions of women to suffer violations of their human rights in the name of perverse traditions makes all of us guilty and partners in crime.

In Simone Weil's essay 'Are We Struggling for Justice?' she declares that humankind has gone mad because of a lack of love. We should focus on love, she advises, if we are to shape a fairer society.

Women who say no

The world is constantly improving for women thanks to the many heroines who challenge their governments and religious leaders in their fight for progress. Amina Afzali, leader of the Afghan Women's Movement, has fought against women wearing the burqa for years, risking her life. Zainab al-Khawaja, a feminist activist from the Arab kingdom of Bahrain, was arrested and imprisoned when she was seven months pregnant for having torn up a picture of King Hamad. Her sister Maryam challenged the authorities by returning from exile to support Zainab and her father when they were both in prison.

Many non-governmental organisations have been created all over the world expressly to advance women's emancipation. Plan International, for instance, motivates girls to distance themselves from violence, such as genital mutilation, early pregnancy and forced marriage, by getting them to join the Because I am a Girl campaign. The help of these NGOs is invaluable, and though governments must do more, luckily many organisations listen to women's voices. America, where the public is very active in supporting such causes, sets an example to the world.

EMILY's List was founded thirty years ago by Ellen Malcolm, a woman determined to support local and federal female candidates. Over the years, this association has grown larger and larger, and contributed to the election of 11 women governors, 18 women senators and 100 female members of Congress. Jenna Lowenstein has worked for EMILY's List for years. She believes that girls have the right to be represented by their government. She is vice president of the digital section, and belongs to the 'dream team' that supported Hillary Clinton in her race for the White House. The women belonging to such groups are all successful in work and life, and are striving to change the world by protecting all women against any kind of discrimination.

It is the mission of these feminist *wonder women* to provide a sort of 'lift' for other women on their way to the higher 'floors' of our society: successful women like Stephanie Hannon, ex-chief technology officer of Hillary for America, who studied at Stanford and Harvard and engineered an artificial knee when she was only sixteen years old; like Amanda Renteria, daughter of Mexican peasants, former basketball champion, student at Harvard and analyst at Goldman Sachs; like Michelle Kwan, champion skater, Disney icon and diplomat at the Asian State Department; or like Wendy Clark, head of marketing at Coca-Cola, who was described by *Fortune* as being one of the most influential women in the world.

Oscar de la Renta, the well-known fashion designer, recently deceased, said, 'We live in an era of globalisation and the era of the woman. Never in the history of the world have women been more in control of their destiny.' We have to heed these words which enshrine the hope of a bright future at last for all the women of the entire world and for the ambitions they aspire to.

We struggle to imagine a different world, yet we need only close our eyes to see courthouses where women in their gowns preside as judges; to see women preaching from a pulpit and celebrating Mass; to see women running hospitals and female deans of colleges debating with men as equals; to see women presidents and diplomats leading our countries and taking decisions guided by maternal wisdom; and to see meetings of women bankers intent on rewriting the standards of the international financial system. All of this is possible. It is the future.

To be born a woman in Italy

In Italy, we lack the political will to prevent violence against women. It has become an increasingly worrying phenomenon. Biological reasons account for deep-seated male aggressiveness: men have a high level of testosterone and their bodies are naturally shaped to attack. But that cannot be a justification. For the sake of the ongoing evolution of the human race, male culture needs to be *reconsidered*.

Over the centuries there has been an endless succession of wars and struggles for power and in every case violence has been the only means of resolution. Religion and politics have established a fighting male role model: the archetype of a warrior ready to subdue those who believe in a different god, or place themselves between him and the Crown. Men's aggressiveness and violent oppression are deeply rooted in our society. It is not surprising that women end up victims.

Sociologist Domenico de Masi uses the term 'alienation' to explain women's lack of awareness of their own rights and to define the conditioning they are subjected to. Male chauvinism dominates their lives so much that the majority of women are passively accepting of all this: they are 'alienated'. I have often asked him why women's condition is especially appalling in Italy: feminicide, domestic violence, unemployment, limited access to power roles and lower salaries than men for equal responsibilities and tasks. How is it possible that one of the seven most developed economies, where 60 per cent of women are graduates, finds itself in such a situation?

The answer lies in our male-dominated culture and in women's very low opinion of themselves. Some of them are aware of this gross social distortion, but think they should look the other way and fight their battle all alone. The lack of solidarity among women worsens the situation.

Female identity is deeply influenced by culture. A woman creates the idea of herself according to what surrounds her. In this respect, Simone de Beauvoir's observation is enlightening: 'One is not born, but becomes a woman. No biological, psychological, or economic fate determines the figure that the human female presents in society: it is civilisation as a whole that produces this creature, intermediate between male and eunuch, which is described as feminine.'

Neither in Italy nor in the wider world, will women ever be able to make it alone. Luckily not all men are part of the problem. We need the good ones to come to grips with the hostile culture their gender has shaped over the centuries. Men have to revolutionise it in the name of a fair and equal society. We in the West are lucky since we have been through the Enlightenment. Brave thinkers fought illiteracy and benighted traditions to stand up for reason. Now it is time for another revolution in thinking.

Violence against women is a social emergency: the government should treat it as one. Feminicide, in particular, is culture-based and can only be tackled at classroom level. Public subsidies for counselling, women's crisis centres, women's shelters, as well as educational projects in primary and secondary schools, training courses for officials, rehabilitation programmes, vocational training, access to work – these are all measures which could transform society in favour of women.

I had the opportunity to discuss the condition of women with the then Italian Minister of Education Stefania Giannini and she agreed with me on the importance of education in preventing violence against women. Following our conversation, she went on to introduce an ad hoc educational path on gender equality in primary and secondary schools. While that particular scheme was not a success in itself due to a public backlash, this surely must be the route we take in future, refining our approach along the way. Our sons and daughters would learn solidarity and respect between genders. In this way, the ideas of mutual love and care – instead of power and ownership – would grow and spread. Our children should know about crimes committed against girls and women in Italy. Thanks to knowledge and memory, human beings can review and reject the wrong behaviour. The reform programme prompted fierce debate, and ultimately those who opposed it managed to put a stop to it, arguing that it promoted a biased gender theory. This says a lot about the dominant conservative culture of the country and how hard it is to change it.

Even in relatively enlightened education systems the 'gender gap' persists. In England, this was the key issue at an international conference. It all started with the petition of a seventeen-year-old girl, Jessy McCabe. This English music student complained about having to study male composers only. She started a campaign led by the most illustrious British girls' schools asking for women who made history in the arts and sciences to be forthwith included in textbooks. Hitherto there had been almost no trace of female geniuses, which suggests that an unconscious prejudice had always existed and influenced billions of students. A syllabus cannot exclude women like Marie Curie, Frida Kahlo and Rita Levi Montalcini, to name but a few.

In Italy such glaring omissions affect all educational resources. What role models can we offer to our girls if women are not mentioned in our school textbooks or at conferences? Such discrimination can even be found in the associations dealing with social policy; the think tanks! During the latest Forum Ambrosetti meeting in Cernobbio, only 14 per cent of the speakers were women: 8 out of 57. Such wilful marginalisation of women's contribution can only perpetuate a deficient, withdrawn culture in which they are incapable of fulfilling their potential.

Gender gap research

A focus on the gender gap has always been at the core of PariMerito's research. What follows is the result of exhaustive and innovative work making use of several search indexes.

The Global Gender Gap Report annually carried out by the WEF (the World Economic Forum) focuses on the gender gap in 142 countries in the areas of the economy, politics, education and health. The primary aim is to enhance awareness of this imbalance and suggest practical ways to reduce it in the different countries.

The report highlights the close correlation between the gender gap in each country and its competitiveness internationally. According to the WEF, women make up half of the potential talent available in each country. And the competitiveness of a country depends significantly on how female talent is encouraged and valued there. Even though a single index cannot easily convey the complexity of the problem, the report ensures we have a realistic picture of the gap between men and women within the four specified main areas.

The 2014 report portrays a marked global improvement in comparison with data from 2006. Northern Europe stays among the very best performing and some Eastern European countries have definitively increased their level of gender equality. However, in the countries ruled by oppressive regimes, women's conditions have worsened. Most of the migrants flowing into Europe come from these countries.

Over the last eight years Italy has moved up from 77th place to 69th in terms of gender equality. However, the change has not been uniform across all areas. Participation in politics increased, starting from 2012 with former Prime Minister Monti, and grew further between 2013 and 2014 with former Prime Ministers Letta and Renzi. More attention is being paid to women's voices thanks to the growing number of female Members of Parliament and women in ministerial office.

But if, on the one hand, Italy has improved in terms of women's political participation raising standards of education and health in the interests of gender equality, on the other our country moves down dramatically in terms of women's participation in the economy and their access to economic opportunities. Equal opportunities in education and health are one thing, but the mechanism gets stuck at entry into the world of work, a recurrent problem in countries which have deficient welfare.

Thanks to PariMerito's tools, and to Director Pasquale Maroni's contribution, we were able to compare the Global Gender Gap with other indexes:

- The Democracy Index: focusing on five categories: electoral process and pluralism; functioning of government; political participation; democratic political culture; and civil liberties. Carried out by *The Economist* (2014)
- The Freedom Index (Freedom in the World): looking at civil liberties and political rights. Carried out by Freedom House (2014)
- The Competitiveness Index: studying economic competitiveness. Carried out by the World Economic Forum (2015)
- The Happiness Index: measuring people's well-being worldwide. Carried out by the Sustainable Development Solutions Network (2015)

The comparison between Global Gender Gap (GGG) and the indexes on Democracy, Freedom, Competitiveness and Happiness was carried out making use of the Spearman index (r), a statistical tool used for measuring the relationship between two ranked variables. The

Spearman index assigns values between -1 and +1. The extremes represent a perfect associative link:

- a value of +1 means that the two variables have a direct relationship (as the first variable increases, the other one increases).
- a value of -1 means that the two variables have an inverse relationship (as the first variable increases, the other one decreases).
- 0 – the intermediate value – means that the two variables are not linked to one another.

The results of the research are as follows:

- GGG v/o Democracy Index: r = +0.57
- GGG v/o Freedom Index: r = +0.52
- GGG v/o Global Competitiveness Index: r = +0.40
- GGG v/o Happiness Index: r = +0.40

In each case, there is a strong correlation between GGG and the index. Hence, in the countries where women's rights are respected, and they can therefore follow independent careers, people live better and the economy grows.

Gender equality is strictly connected to the Democracy Index rating of each country. One influences the other. However, another strong correlation is apparent in the results of our research: one between competitiveness and global happiness. Obviously, the countries in which competitiveness grows despite the gender gap, such as the United Arab Emirates and Qatar, are the exceptions to the rule. Here the economy is strictly connected to raw materials like petroleum and gas.

In view of the above, we may conclude that gender equality is fundamental to a country's economy. Only the economies that have full access to the talents of both men and women are competitive and prosperous.

Healthy and educated women are more likely to raise healthy and educated children – a positive cycle with a real impact on the community. When the number of women who actively participate in politics and economic affairs increases, their decisions lead to more far-reaching results. At a lower level – in terms of economic structure, not of relevance – all this is reflected in the success of individual companies as well: the firms hiring women and conferring upon them leadership roles according to principles of meritocracy and equality increase their profits more than the companies not paying attention to diversity.

Preventing the gender gap

Countering the gender gap does not only mean educating the young but also training the adults who work on a daily basis with victims of abuse and domestic violence: local authorities, doctors, lawyers, magistrates, judges. How is it possible that in Palermo, in 2015, a trial for rape was halted and the victim grilled as if she were guilty of what had happened to her? Rapes often go unreported because victims dread having to face such humiliation. In 1973, the actress Franca Rame, Dario Fo's memorable partner, was kidnapped and raped by five masked men. Even a woman like her who had always been active in the campaign for women's rights hesitated to report the rape. A trial was held twenty-five years later, in spite of the lapse of time.

Fighting to eradicate violence against women means fighting against the fear to speak up as well: rapes and abuses must be reported and not suffered in silence. In 2015, a campaign against domestic violence was launched in the USA: the Black Dot Campaign. The victims of violence and abuse incapable of reporting their partners were invited to draw a black dot on the palm of their hand. A signal, an SOS, a code asking for help from those who could stand up for them. Another important demonstration of solidarity to those women who do not have the courage or the strength to expose their oppressors.

A prime example of patriarchal culture and women's alienation is an episode that happened in the countryside near Pesaro, Italy. Igli, an Albanian boy who had grown up in Italy, killed another boy, sixteen-year-old Ismaele, because he dared court Ambera, Igli's girlfriend. Instead of being horrified, the girl declared herself to be madly in love with Igli. According to Ambera, Igli fought for the sake of love, and she could not condemn him. This attitude takes us back in time to an era when honour crimes were common law!

If Igli and Ambera were simply following the teaching of the *Kanun*, the code of the culture to which they belong, according to that text a wife's father has to provide his son-in-law with a dowry, together with a bullet to use against the wife in case she dares disobey or betray him. Article 28 of the *Kanun* states that women's blood cannot be compared with men's blood.

If we do not re-educate the young who have been born and raised amongst tyranny and violent traditions to respect women, no progress shall ever be made. They must learn that in our countries integration requires understanding and respect for women's rights. We have to teach them the value of the goals we have struggled to reach. Such goals have to be defended and nourished with love.

Education is the most powerful weapon we have. But it will not be enough in itself. The government has to support women's shelters and foster homes which currently struggle to survive on meagre financial assistance from the state. These centres do valuable work for our society, but are left alone to tackle what is a grave social emergency. Women who have suffered from abuse often go there with their children: they need to be rehabilitated and reintegrated into society, if possible by being trained for a job so that they can start working and become economically self-sufficient. We need an all-female Marshall Plan, with specific and considerable subsidies for such structures. These would be funds for the future of the world; for its salvation. Without such measures, violence will grow. The women victims of abuse will not know to whom they can appeal and will give up reporting. And new victims will crowd the statistics we read carelessly every day. What are we waiting for?

If we want to break the chain of abuse, we will have to invest in women, help them to believe in themselves and provide them with the tools to improve their education and become aware of their rights. Freeing women is fundamental: they can save our planet. International politics, diplomacy and economic relations among countries; all should be based on a new awareness. To quote Emmeline Pankhurst, 'We have to free half of the human race, the women, so that they can help to free the other half.'

It is possible. Provided we have the will.

5
To Be a Woman in England

'Life without freedom is like a body without a soul.'

Kahlil Gibran

Build your own mountain

I am in love with London. It is pure energy, oxygen. Here, I breathe in optimism and positive thinking, exhaling them all around me in elation at the rediscovery of a global society which can, and must, initiate change. I love it not only because of the incredible opportunities the city offers to those who choose to live here. Not only for the blend of cultures and nationalities. But also, and most of all, for the extraordinary women I meet here every day. London is a beating heart from which possibilities for the future permeate throughout England and beyond.

Women's history is the same in all countries: marked by submission and a denial of rights. Even in those areas where all human rights are trampled, women's condition is always the most intractable. We suffer the most. We get humiliated, reduced to slavery, accused and condemned to unacceptable living conditions by husbands, fathers and brothers. I remember the story of a friend, a well-known anthropologist, journalist and university lecturer who was born and raised in Africa. She told me that, after a trip to Europe, she went back to her country laden with suitcases and presents. When her sisters, her brother and her mother came to pick her up at the station, her sisters busied themselves with carrying the luggage while her brother stood hands-free. Loading women with heavy burdens was normal in their culture!

In England, as in Italy, women have been subservient to the dominant male culture for centuries. As a result we have become objects instead of subjects, we have been enslaved to family needs and hidden away in domestic quarters. Family is a basic need, but it is sometimes incompatible with the possibility of being fulfilled, free and unique. As we were born.

Today we can finally be ourselves. We are not socially acknowledged only as wives, mothers, daughters and sisters. Unfortunately, this cannot yet be said for all the women in the world. Cities like London showcase precious living gems, 'feminine diamonds' who shine by their own light and illuminate the path for others. They can be found in organisations like The Sorority, the network founded by entrepreneur Lisa Tse; an extraordinarily talented woman who, starting from scratch, has created two successful companies and a global members club made up of exceptional women. They are businesswomen, managers, artists, philanthropists, passionate people who try to better themselves every day and are not fazed by the inevitable obstacles put in the way of women, especially successful women.

When we were talking about our roots and shared experiences of discrimination, Lisa told me about a mountain in China that had been inherited by her brother. I asked her, 'Did you not claim your share?' She looked at me and answered, seraphic and proud, 'I do not want to argue. I will build my own mountain!' I think her reply encapsulates the independence and strength of soul that are an example to us all: they are qualities not only belonging to Lisa, but to many women living in the UK who strive together for global emancipation and women's rights. Each woman must build her own mountain in order to climb it for herself.

Every day I meet women of different nationalities but with the same ideals; multiculturalism is added value. They come from all continents. They are extraordinarily intelligent, hungry for personal and professional fulfilment, alive, full of intent. They meet here to share and celebrate the joys of progress, meritocracy and opportunity; essential elements on the road to success for a businesswoman like me, who is neither the daughter, nor the wife, nor the sister of someone important.

London, in being a place to mix with free, strong, emancipated, working and business women, is an inexhaustible source of inspiration. London is not an earthly paradise, since inequalities still exist, but here there are top female representatives making their voices heard and trying to bridge the gender gap. In Italy, as in other countries, not many women at the top fight for others to join them, maybe because the 'social lift' is stuck, especially the women's one. The majority of women politicians owe their appointments to men and do not have a deep gender awareness and most of the businesswomen have inherited the companies they are leading. Nothing wrong with that, but meeting them is less stimulating than meeting the founders of new companies, which have often been launched with neither economic help, nor political compromise. Creativity and business skills at maximum power are what you need if you are founding something new. What's more, if you have climbed the mountain and risked falling many times, have avoided slipping into the clutches of male chauvinism and nepotism, once at the top you feel it natural to help other women climb. You throw ropes of useful information and advice, you break the chain of indifference.

The golden rule is not to give up; to get back on your feet after each fall stronger than before. Hold on to the ideals you have made the foundation of your life. Personality, courage, inner strength, ambition: in the meritocratic British society such qualities are a prerogative for women; there is no question of following the example of other countries that 'educate' girls to be modest and to not ask too much from themselves or, most of all, from men.

Nowadays, girls not only have to build their own mountain, but they must also learn to fly, to be strong, to not make do with what they have in life but to instead seek fulfilment. The path towards emancipation from imposed male stereotypes might start with wasting less time in front of a mirror and spending more time reading a good book. Living just to please men and depending on a husband to allow you a more satisfactory quality of life is wrong. You are a mine; you contain all the treasure of the universe. Do not let false myths, poor ideals and cultural conditioning rob you of your potential. It is true that when a woman is independent she finds it difficult to meet a man who respects her, supports her, devotes more time to family care. Perhaps the problem is that men are not ready for gender equality. They are not emotionally and managerially independent, since they have been educated to expect the privilege of a woman who will provide care without the requirement of understanding and support in return. This one-way dependence is damaging to themselves, the education of their children and the fulfilment of their partners.

The 'traditional' institution of marriage is destined to break down if it does not change. A balance between the partners must be arrived at. Women cannot be subjugated to the male command, nor turned into robots or cynical alpha females. We have to create conditions that help couples to live a full and satisfactory life, sharing love and pursuing careers on equal terms. Thank God that men exist who are willing to practise this equality in their relationships and one can only hope that this is on the way to becoming the new norm.

On an epochal level, we are caught between two tectonic plates crashing into each other. One is the patriarchal tradition; the other is the future when we will have equal rights and equal duties. In such a collision, it is difficult to keep your balance. Stability can come from solidarity, not only among women but also with the men whom I call 'enlightened'; the ones who support women's emancipation and consider it something precious for them and their children.

In England, everything can start anew on any given day and reach the rest of the world, changing it forever. The working-class women responsible for gaining equal rights at work were employed at the Ford factory in Dagenham. Rose Boland, Sheila Douglass, Violet Dawson and the others. While sewing car seats, they started wondering why men were paid better. On 7 June 1968, just fifty years ago (the historical chronology is alarming when you consider how recently there were no regulations or rights), the women started a three-week strike which brought production to a standstill. Managers, trade unions and male colleagues were all against them. Only another woman offered her support: Secretary of State for Employment Barbara Castle, who formulated the Equal Pay Act, a law for equal rights at work. Until then the workers did not know how strong they were.

This is why I am writing this book; because I truly believe that it is women who can bring about change at this moment in history. The women at Dagenham, holding on to their beliefs, climbed not only their own mountain, but changed the social order, rearranging the puzzle. These women gave a chance to all the others. It is up to us to continue their work. Never take for granted such important achievements: they have been attained by sacrifice and courage. And there is still a great deal to be done.

My need to publish *Saving the World* in England, as well as in Italy, comes from the bitter awareness that although British women's condition is more advanced than that of others along the path to gender equality, it has stopped halfway. A lot has been done, especially in the last hundred years, but there is still a great distance to travel. To maintain a successful career and a close family is often an impossible dream. Marriage, work and children can often be incompatible or discouragingly difficult to combine. Today, women are still forced to choose between love and work. Many of us opt for economic self-sufficiency instead of a 'man-centred' love life, yet experience an inner struggle and end up raising our children on our own. This is often because our partners face us with a choice between being mothers and wives or independent women, without saying it in so many words – they deliver a veiled diktat, made of gestures, absence and a lack of support.

Freedom is a basic human necessity but it should not be at odds with marriage and motherhood. Freedom actually promotes and enhances such conditions. We are perfectly capable of succeeding in every role life offers us.

The prostitute poet

Aphra Behn (1640–1689) was the first British woman to become a professional writer. She turned rules inside out, overcame obstacles thought insurmountable and won the fight for equality with unprecedented courage. She wrote under her own name, spurning the yoke of a male pseudonym, a device used by women in that period to publish their work. Male critics appraised her with disdain, trying to darken her literary purity and uncontrollable talent and dubbing her the 'prostitute poet'.

The term prostitute is an insult applied only to women. But behind the real or metaphorical act it implies, so degrading for a woman, behind the moral and ethical debasement, there is a paying man, often a married man. Herein lies a paradox.

I explained to my children why they should not say the word 'prostitute'. It is a disparaging term coined by men who despise women's sexual freedom and resent them being on an equal footing. A man having sex with more than one woman is a Latin lover. A woman who has sex with several men is a prostitute. Harems and brothels are men's inventions. We get used and paid by men who first exploit us and then despise us, annihilating our personality.

For whom did Aphra Behn write her texts? Who were her customers, readers, critics? If they had been women, she would not have gone down in history with the epithet 'prostitute of literature' but for the variety of her themes, her original style and the courage of her convictions.

Among the many rights denied, one has always been recognised by brave women: the right to cause offence to men by going against their expectations. By doing so, a woman could then sell her intelligence. The acknowledgement and praise of a woman's genius comparable to William Shakespeare's, that of Aphra Behn's, was too much to ask in the seventeenth century. However, one other great woman would do it, three hundred years later: Virginia Woolf. The rooms of culture, inaccessible to sensitivity and feminine genius since time immemorial, were finally opened to the dignity of a woman who claimed a room of her own.

A Room of One's Own, written by Virginia Woolf in 1928, is an essay based on two lectures read at Cambridge University in the women's colleges Newnham and Girton. It is an adventurous and painful journey through the history of women's travails in literature. Woolf screamed softly into the gentle ears of Cambridge girls that it was time to acknowledge that women are as skilful as men, in all respects. She used the example of Behn to prove that women have been capable of equalling men for hundreds of years.

The talented young women of a society such as Britain's, still deeply patriarchal at the time, were the best audience. Culture had been the preserve of waistcoats and cigars for too long. 'Let me imagine, since facts are so hard to come by, what would have happened had Shakespeare had a wonderfully gifted sister, called Judith, let us say…'

Reference to Aphra Behn is explicit. Judith, the protagonist, has two alternatives: either to become a writer and pay the price by being excluded, or to give in to her father's will and get married. The story does not have a happy end. Woolf has the protagonist commit suicide in order to demonstrate to her audience just how tragic the plight of creative women has been. Judith, as us all, cannot submit and become a slave. But she cannot become free either. Woolf shed light on the dark side of women's condition; the ideals and imperatives imposed by men. Judith suffers on two counts: society does not acknowledge her and she is subjected to her father's tyranny. He wants her to embrace the roles of wife and mother: the fulfilment of these roles are the only rights she is entitled to. Children, the household and marriage often have negative connotations for Woolf, since they risk becoming an excuse; a pretext used by women to avoid necessary change.

In contrast with Shakespeare, her brother, the father of English literature, we have Judith the mother, who is confined to her rooms for much of the year. Aphra Behn is the female writers' mother, the first one who managed to get paid in order to be read. The first one who combined existential, intellectual and economic freedom. In spite of the marginalisation and the violence she was subjected to, she did not give up and was renumerated on a regular basis for her work.

Shakespeare's imaginary sister, conversely, is prevented from following her literary inclinations. She cannot study, nor do the same things her brother does. She is not treated like him. She runs away from home in order not to deny herself. But she dies.

Woolf's vision of a room of one's own is a middle ground between the rooms of the house where women were segregated and the rooms of high culture they had no access to. It is a room of our own, free women! Judith's story must not and cannot be perpetuated: this is what Woolf set out to impress on young British women's minds. Today, I wonder when global consciousness will change and accept a common entity with equal rights: the human being. At all times, in all latitudes, extraordinarily talented and brave women have existed. But in every age, and in every part of the world, such women have had to struggle for their basic rights and keep fighting to retain them. For thousands of years we have paid with our lives for wanting to be who we are. Women of every social background get killed throughout the world, every day, by their husbands, fathers and brothers. Like new martyrs in a never-ending cycle. Lambs sacrificed on the altar of emancipation. Virgins as well as fertile mothers: mothers of a new humankind.

Maybe it is thanks to Aphra Behn first and then to Virginia Woolf – who, as perhaps the most famous member of the Bloomsbury Group, active in the fields of the arts, criticism and teaching, inspired the most receptive female minds – that I am able to write, with conviction, women, you are saving the world.

Women writing

Writing has long been a man's profession. Women weren't encouraged to study or attend cultural and artistic establishments. A wealth of talent was lost. Up to the nineteenth century, publishing a book was so inconceivable for a woman that three Victorian sisters, Anne, Charlotte and Emily Brontë, assumed the names Acton, Currer and Ellis Bell. They knew prejudice would have denied success to their work if they had published their real names and they were brilliant in planning a literary disguise. But changing a feminine sensibility requires much more than a name. And if *Jane Eyre* gained the critics' approval, *Wuthering Heights* did not; and *The Tenant of Wildfell Hall*, in which the protagonist runs away from an unhappy marriage, was condemned for its offensive and inappropriate content and language. Charlotte Bronte, whose alias was Currer Bell, explained the thinking behind their pseudonyms: 'Averse to personal publicity, we veiled our own names under those of Currer, Ellis and Acton Bell; that ambiguous choice being dictated by a sort of conscientious scruple at assuming Christian names positively masculine, while we did not like to declare ourselves women, because – without at that time suspecting that our mode of writing and thinking was not what is called "feminine" we had a vague impression that authoresses are liable to be looked on with prejudice.' In 1847 *Wuthering Heights* was a big success in terms of readers, but Emily could not enjoy fame: instead, Ellis Bell could. Only after her death, when Charlotte published the novel with the real name of the author, did things begin to change in the consciousness of Britain and the world.

Two centuries later, women can sign their masterpieces! As previously mentioned, *Harry Potter*'s author Joanne Rowling has long been open about how her publisher advised her to hide her female identity with the initials J.K., arguing that boys do not like reading books written by a woman. She, who used to write at a cafe table for want of a better desk, kept the strength of her gender even if recognition of her womanhood was lacking. Starting from scratch, she produced one of the most important masterpieces of the fantasy genre, destined to go down in history. The celebrated wizard was created by a single and impecunious mother. That's the secret of the philosopher's stone: do not give up. And I wish the gift of perseverance to all women in difficult conditions. A spell that could only be made in a magic country; in England where everything is still possible.

We unquestionably need to be magical, not only to be determined enough to succeed in our profession within a man's world, but also to raise ourselves from the ruins of personal setbacks, almost always caused by male authority, the male authority that daily devastates the lives of women in some corner of the planet.

Rowling, besides creating the most popular character of current literature, filling the bookshops of the whole world with millions of people and having an all-time box-office smash hit for fifteen years, did something even braver: she founded a charity, Lumos, named after Harry's magic formula. The light-creation spell is exactly what we need if we are to achieve an enormous objective a real home and a real family for all the children in the world.

It all started with a picture in a magazine of a child locked in a cage. Unfortunately, confining children in this way is common in many countries afflicted with the increasing phenomenon of poor abandoned children. Lumos is active in Czechia, Ukraine, Bulgaria, Moldova, the USA and Great Britain. It aims to eliminate the need for orphanages and group homes over the next twenty years. Eight million children are at present in childcare facilities in these countries. Rowling has launched a global challenge of staggering ambition. Out-of-the-ordinary women like her baffle not only men but also the imagination.

One century ago, Agatha Christie became the best-selling writer of all time, besides Shakespeare. Her books have sold more than two billion copies and been translated into fifty languages in spite of her using a female name. Christie was a one-step-ahead British woman and we can only marvel at her originality and literary invulnerability. First *Poirot*, then *Miss Marple* reached unprecedented popularity. Much later, another feminine icon, Angela Lansbury, performed a character inspired by Miss Marple. Not only a single woman, but also a widow, Jessica Fletcher became an icon of independence, wit, genius and irony who gained worldwide success. Again, a detective story is tinged with pink. Jessica Fletcher solves almost three hundred murder cases and has become a reference point for all and an icon of popular culture. The original idea was to make a TV series about Miss Marple, but Christie's heirs would not assign the rights. So, the authors created a similar character: the widow of Cabot Cove, in Maine, who tracks down murderers and writes detective stories. Angela Lansbury, who had already played Miss Marple in a film, became the protagonist of *Murder, She Wrote* in 1984; it was to be a triumph for thirty years.

English literature has been a platform for revolutionary women like Christie because of their courage and will to succeed on behalf of all women. Doris Lessing, very dear to me, had women's interests in her blood. The Royal Swedish Academy, when awarding her the Nobel Prize for Literature in 2007, described her as an epic narrator of the feminine experience. *The Grass is Singing* (1950) and *The Golden Notebook* (1962) became manifestos of the women's movement, even though she did not mean to support feminism. Instead, over the years she made it quite clear that she disliked being called a feminist. She was a writer for everyone and didn't want to identify with, or be restricted to, what she considered a stereotype. However, she argued that in her life she had never met a woman who was not feminist in essence, implying that the two words are synonymous. Hence, to be a woman means to be a feminist even if you do not feel like one.

For Mary Shelley feminism was a birthright. She was the daughter of feminist pioneer Mary Wollstonecraft, who wrote *A Vindication of the Rights of Women* in 1792, and of William Godwin, a political writer who did not think in the same way as his wife in terms of women but acknowledged and supported his daughter's genius and personality after her mother's death. Mary Shelley was incompatible with her father's second spouse, so he sent her to live with some radical friends. This was an opportunity for Mary who, in tune with her new family, could express herself and avoid adapting to the dominant culture. Her personality strengthened: she wrote such 'masculine' work that critics were unable to assign it to a woman. *Frankenstein*, anonymously published in 1818, was declared by critics to have been written by her husband, Percy Shelley, who contributed its preface.

Her love for her husband was a constant in Mary's life; so much so that she kept his heart in a drawer after his death. On the first anniversary of her death, Mary's son and daughter-in-law found a copy of the poem 'Adonais' in her desk, along with a silk tissue containing the remains of Percy's heart. It is said that, during the cremation of Mary's husband, who had died years before, his heart did not burn and was delivered to her. The story is an emblem of what great English women writers represented deep within themselves and in their masterpieces, of how they contributed to changing the predominant culture. From Jane Austen to Mary Shelley, they all had the courage to embrace their womanhood and to live their love stories in front of millions of readers.

The women of English literature have not only helped all other women to feel kinship but they have also shown the world that their desire to feel loved and their tendency to feel chagrin when not respected are normal. They taught us that we have the right to be loved entirely and that it is normal to oppose the unequal standards between men and women regarding what constitutes a betrayal. They gave value to all of us through the portrayal of their characters. Jane Austen's women, for example, are always at the core of her work; different individually but with something in common, like all of us. The writer is her own women; we are them and her. They have faces, bodies, styles, personalities, moods and, most of all, hearts. Talking about Elizabeth Bennet, from *Pride and Prejudice*, Austen said that she thought Elizabeth the most exquisite character ever described in a book and that she could not stand those who did not like her.

The sense of sympathy and universal communion among women that readers experience explains the timeless success of these early novelists' masterpieces. I say thanks to them all for the right to express myself today. And it is also thanks to their pioneering spirit that I can now publish my ideas under my own name: I do not need to use the name of one of my relatives. With their work, British women writers crossed all barriers of language, culture, social status and gender; they are the ancestors of the young women finding their voices today. If you truly believe in dreams and you are ready to fight for them, they will finally come true.

Thanks also to these writers for having understood men's thoughts and told them with a woman's heart. They have awakened men's ability to love, suffer, make mistakes and, most of all, apologise. We grew up without even noticing how big an influence on our world their books were. We do not talk enough about what women's sensitivity has produced over time, about how women's contribution has helped to civilise the world, about how much our cultural evolution owes to women who wrote, painted, composed, sang and created.

Love is a woman

Regardless of geographical position or cultural sophistication, from emancipated areas of the planet to the most isolated provinces, women have always been deemed of less worth than men. In the past, worth was equated with physical strength. Do we need to learn to use strength? Yes, we do: the strength of thinking, of personality, of determination and willpower. That is the truth: our strength lies in being ourselves, if we do not get killed for it, since our emancipation starts again from scratch every day, as we can see from the worldwide data on feminicide.

Let us take inspiration from the women who first loved freely. The ones who first had the courage to show their bodies. The ones who first believed in the dream of the right to education and to work – since such things are a dream to those deprived of what is normal to others. 'My inferior condition must be by divine decree or because

I have a deficiency of some sort,' is what our great-grandmothers, grandmothers and mothers must have thought sometimes, and countless women are still forced to think so, every day.

Every moment many of us take a step closer to universal emancipation. Yes, today we are worth as much as our brothers, we make decisions on our own or together with our fathers. But the mechanism is a big oscillating engine: many of us live in countries where we still cannot dress as we like. Where men are free and hold powerful and prestigious positions but not women; they are victims of oppression and violence just because they want something more. England should take the lead in delivering the global community from the toxic cloud of tyrannical male chauvinism.

Sometimes there are men who stand up, who make sacrifices for a woman, even if that means losing money, prestige and power. Edward VIII felt that he would not be able to fulfil his duties as king without the help and support of the woman he loved. That was what he said when he renounced his claim to the Crown of England. He abdicated for the love of divorcee, Wallis Simpson. The two fell in love against the wishes of King George and Queen Mary, who did not welcome Wallis at Buckingham Palace as a result of their disapproval. When his father died, Edward became King of England. But one year later, he chose to abdicate in order to be with Wallis. The new king was George VI, his brother. Edward took the title Duke of Windsor and married Wallis who, as the Duchess of Windsor, stood by him for thirty-five years. A lot was written about this story, but no amount of reportage, scandal or gossip could cast doubt on the strength of his love for Mrs Simpson.

This extraordinary episode demonstrates that a powerful man is not only capable of considering his partner as an equal, but also of leaving everything behind for love's sake. Something similar happened long after to another famous British figure: John Lennon. As soon as he first met Yoko Ono, he fell under her spell. She was seen as the wicked witch and was blamed for eclipsing Lennon's image and undermining his role in The Beatles but John and Yoko refused to be cowed by the negative publicity.

These are both examples of how a man can, and must, acknowledge a woman's value. We tend to put men first, at least until they tear us apart: 'His idea was still with me, because it was not a vapour sunshine could disperse, nor a sand-traced effigy storms could wash away; it was a name graven on a tablet, fated to last as long as the marble it inscribed,' to quote Jane Eyre on Mr Rochester. This passage refers to women's attitude to love and the value we give to men. But it should work both ways.

As a result of the caring nature of women, hundreds of charitable organisations have sprung up all over the world. They are supported by women from all walks of life. We have a genetic inclination to take care of others, to give our all. Otherwise, Nature would not have assigned us the role of carrying and feeding the next generation, risking our lives to give birth. Human life comes from women's readiness to offer up their bodies, their biological independence and their free movement. It is a natural virtue. Our womb is a gift and the physical emblem of our ability to nurture life, shield it and guide its first steps in the world.

In Great Britain, and most of all in London, I see a proliferation of charities active on behalf of different causes

– children, the homeless, the disabled, refugees, etc. This is much more apparent than in the rest of Europe.

The UK invests in the sector not only with money, but also in terms of time, in a most natural way. It is a typical feature of British society. I wish all the world could have it. I notice that in other countries people are less interested in the public good. They feel exempted from sharing the global discomfort. But we cannot say we are free until all of us are free. We are all one since we are all humankind. I am reminded of the parable Jesus told of the widow who gave her last coin to the poor. He considered it a huge fortune since it was all the woman had. To give, in however small a way, makes a difference.

I support many charities; mainly those focused on helping women and children. One of these is Womankind, a global organisation for women's rights based in London which is supporting various movements in Africa with the same aim. With almost three decades of experience, Womankind moves ever closer to a world where all women's rights have been won and are respected and protected. It is a practical example of feminist diplomacy aiming to help developing countries and their economic progress.

There is still so much to do to help women around the world. While in one country a woman can be prime minister, somewhere else another cannot even express her opinions without suffering violent abuse. There is a video on YouTube, repeatedly played on International Women's Day, which shows a woman sitting behind her husband. When he starts singing a traditional Arabic chant and she corrects him, the man stands up, beats her and the woman is forced to leave the house. Male guests are sneering in the background. Only a girl, presumably the daughter, goes and helps her mother, but both of them have to remain on the threshold; they cannot come back in, otherwise they will be beaten again. This scene is daily life for many women. At the same time, on the other side of the world, women rule not only their homes but whole countries. An alarming dichotomy: one woman is elected president, another one is denied her right to exist. We all have a duty to bridge this gap, this moral and cultural void where inequality flourishes.

I am sure that healing will come, at least for future generations, if women have strong role models: inspiring images of those who have made good life choices; figures of women who have made and are making history; icons of beauty, most of all of inner beauty, who have taken control of their lives through sheer determination. If we are to bring about the great revolution we must make the journey, accomplish the mission; we must engender universal love and respect in the world, starting by nurturing a love and respect for ourselves and all women.

The essential has become visible to our eyes: the Queen and others

Queen Elizabeth II sets an example to all women. She is not a feminist icon; in her role as monarch she has not been in a position to actively fight for women's rights; her people would not have wanted her to defy the constitution. But she stays a revolutionary woman, who, without doubt, welcomes women's rights as a fundamental priority of the nation. Elizabeth embodies the subtle essence of feminism and has, over sixty-five years, conducted herself with style and authoritativeness on the world stage.

The Queen has demonstrated that women should never be underestimated. She has fulfilled her role as well as, if not better than, any man. She has faced difficult events in her personal life with unfailing dignity. Family tragedies, such as death, illness and divorce, are as painful for a Queen as for a commoner.

We know the Queen of England through her public life, and guess at her opinions of the prime ministers who have served under her. But to get to know the woman behind her crown, we need to put ourselves in her place. She never agrees to interviews that might seek to probe her feelings, fears, inner struggles and womanhood. Seventy years of marriage and we still do not know anything about Philip's possible betrayal. But Elizabeth, with her own personality, transcends our curiosity about royal gossip: what we are really interested in is her. Whatever the truth as to the rumoured betrayal, she has taken it in her stride and successfully preserved her marriage for seventy years. Long marriages are perhaps anachronistic nowadays, even for royal couples: Charles and Diana, Sarah and Andrew; divorce is now routine at court. Royal or not, it seems that divorce goes hand in hand with women's emancipation, that marriage stood as long as women could stand it! Parents, a husband, children, daughters-in-law, sons-in-law, grandchildren and now great-grandchildren, the Queen, has coped with everything and has always stood by them all. An attitude shared by every woman of her times: each faithful and royal in their own small way. Dignity, strength, the ability to stand by and remain silent.

Elizabeth's story tells of how a woman, a most visible and important one, has stood at the top without the slightest *défaillance* for more than half a century. When she was eighteen, she was already a Counsellor of State. She stood by the King and with her youthful wisdom influenced his decisions. During World War II, Elizabeth was trained to drive lorries and fix engines. She persuaded her father to let her play an active part as she believed she had to make a contribution. She joined the Auxiliary Territorial Service and became number 230873, Second Subaltern Elizabeth Windsor. Months later, due to her commitment, perseverance and zeal she was promoted to Junior Honorary Commander.

Her strong personality, her courage, as well as her will to challenge herself and not spare any effort, were to stand her in good stead. In 1951, during a journey around the world, from Kenya to Australia and passing through Canada, she received the news that her father had died. She was just twenty-five when she ascended to the throne. Her coronation was broadcast by the BBC and for the first time in history they were able to transmit the images to European networks. Elizabeth was unconsciously spearheading a silent feminist revolution, appearing on the pages of all newspapers, and being broadcast across the world.

As head of state she was also the head of the Anglican Church and in 1961 was the first British monarch to pay a visit to the Pope in the Vatican. She represented not only the British monarchy but the institution of monarchy itself. During her famous speech in Cape Town on her twenty-first birthday, she declared, 'My whole life, whether it be long or short, shall be devoted to your service, and the service of our great imperial family to which we all belong.' She has kept her word.

Belief in her birthright is not enough to guarantee a woman's success. Not even boldness, personality, talent.

Not even if she comes from an illustrious and wealthy family – even a royal one. She always has to invent something new. Otherwise doors will not open. The extraordinary example of Elizabeth I demonstrates how a woman who is shrewd enough can dare to cross gender boundaries. Beyond expectation, she found herself queen, and in order to maintain a steady hold on power she chose not to marry, preferring to remain the 'Virgin Queen'. The brilliance of her strategy was acknowledged by her people, who otherwise would have barely understood her choice to stay single. Consequently, a single woman ruled and ensured prosperity and stability to her subjects for forty-five years.

The British monarchy pioneered women's emancipation, shaping a collective consciousness less grounded in the ideology of male chauvinism. Powerful women planted their seeds in England centuries ago, and have since produced redoubtable leaders such as Margaret Thatcher, the Iron Lady. She did not come from a privileged background, as previous leaders of her party had done, but she changed Britain in historically and politically crucial times. As the first woman prime minister, she crashed through the glass ceiling but allowed it to be re-glazed over the heads of all other women. Thatcher did not directly fight for the establishment of a gender-balanced ruling class. She was not a 'lift' woman, one of my favourite metaphors for women who raise other women up to their level. She declared that feminism was poison. As a champion of meritocracy, she kept on believing that ability was the only useful requirement, regardless of gender.

Modern social science estimates that meritocracy on its own would produce equality between men and women in developed countries within a century, and within two in developing countries. Hence, 'affirmative action' providing support to women is required to accelerate the process. This is the measure of how entrenched discrimination is.

Margaret Thatcher, who reached the top of the political tree, may not have pressed the women's issue with declarations and opinions, but her very existence, as well as Elizabeth II's, achieved the revolution. History can never deny that two women ruled England from the end of the 1970s to the beginning of the 1990s. They were imprinted as role models on young women's consciousness at a time when women were looking for their own social status and personality. Their existence means that a girl has been able to dream of becoming prime minister for the last forty years. Even today, this is still an impossible dream in many countries.

A comparison with Theresa May comes naturally here. Like Mrs Thatcher, she has a middle-class background but, differing from her, May believes in the duty to help other women forge their careers. She supports women at Westminster, caring for their rights, although she could do more.

We must list other examples, since our goal of equal opportunities has not yet been fully realised and it is still uncommon to see women holding top jobs. Girls living in the UK are luckier than others, they are used to seeing a multitude of women in leading positions. Nicola Sturgeon, Scottish Prime Minister, has been the leader of the Scottish National Party since 2014, but notably she is the first woman to hold both offices. Harriet Harman, in Parliament since 1982, former Leader of the Opposition, is another great example. These are the sort of trailblazers we need if women are to achieve their potential. Each of them is a model to follow; ultimate success will not come from one of them, nor from some of them, but will come from a critical mass of women reaching the top in key sectors across the world. Each of us is a seed. Even if a woman remains invisible and underground for a time, one day she will become a strong tree with roots powerful enough to break through prejudices and conventions. We cannot call ourselves civilised until there is gender equality in every corner of the earth.

According to research carried out in Europe over recent years, gender discrimination against women is still appallingly common and especially in the world of work, where women from all countries reported its ubiquity. The percentage of women who claimed to have faced sexual discrimination in their professional environment was higher than 50 per cent everywhere. Salaries are lower, access to prestigious positions is limited. Making a career is more difficult. It seems women need to struggle twice or three times more forcefully than men to achieve the same results. We learn to do it. And to pretend it comes naturally to us. It is a fierce battle. To win we need to be armed with weapons like out-of-the-ordinary personality and talent. And what about those who do not own or cannot acquire such weapons? All of us, every day, have to expect sexual abuse, indecent proposals, humiliation and degrading treatment, whether we are waitresses, artists, entrepreneurs or anything else. That is why we need to raise our eyes and get inspired by the extraordinary women who have won through and who are currently fighting for us.

Baroness Cox is now over eighty, but she still travels the world on humanitarian missions. A long-serving British politician appointed baroness by the Queen, she has sat in the House of Lords for more than thirty years. Her foundation, the Humanitarian Aid Relief Trust (HART), supports the weakest among the weak in areas other charities or aid workers find it hard to reach: countries with a high level of privation.

The baroness is currently fighting for the approval of a draft law prohibiting the sexual discrimination carried out by British Sharia courts. A Sharia court is a legal court in the UK where disputes among citizens following the Islamic faith are settled according to Islamic Law. The baroness is concerned that Sharia law is applied too widely in Great Britain, foregrounding Islamic culture and often replacing British law. *The Times* estimates that roughly 100,000 Muslims in Great Britain are married according to Sharia law and that a high percentage of these marriages are polygamous. Many Muslim women get systematically oppressed, abused and discriminated against all over England. Baroness Cox's forty-page report asserts that women are forced to appear before Sharia courts, rather than civil ones, by means of threats and intimidation. The second, third and fourth wives are not protected by British law because as far as the law is concerned, their marital status simply does not exist. But we do not know how many of them are aware of it. In fact, many of them become aware of the bitter truth when it is too late. According to Baroness Cox, Sharia courts are creating a parallel legal system that is oppressing Muslim women. The baroness leads a brave campaign in the name of all women's rights, whatever religion they belong to, and is not deterred by the fear of clashing with the politically correct lobby. I totally agree with this fight. It is deeply unfair that behind the shield of religion, violations of women's rights occur; such as forced marriages, child marriages, polygamy and sexual violence within marriage. I believe a country like Great Britain should make women's rights a priority and place them before all other economic, religious and political interests. To wash our hands like Pontius Pilate of women's suffering is not acceptable in an advanced society.

Baroness Scotland is another staunch reformer whose changes to the law in the UK have contributed to reducing domestic violence by 64 per cent. According to Scotland, the largest percentage of violence occurs in the home and is often inflicted by the people the victims care most for. This is never adequately reported. Born Dominican, she moved to the UK when she was a child. She was the first black woman to become Attorney General, a post held by white men for centuries. Fierce in her defence of women, she points out that a country's wealth resides in its people, a resource diminished and undermined by such travesties as domestic violence.

Scotland recalls that when she was young, before being a lawyer, some people used to tell her that 'women like you' would find it difficult to establish themselves. She used to answer, 'What do you mean by women like me? The socialists? The Catholics? My fellow citizens? People who were not educated in expensive private schools?' It was a way to place in an uncomfortable position those who were trying to do that very thing to her, a black woman. They needed to be confronted with their own ignorance.

Baroness Scotland stresses that domestic violence occurs at all levels of society. During a journey to Paris with two women from the French government and a journalist, Baroness Scotland happened to say that one woman out of four is a victim of domestic violence and that, since she and her companions were four, one of them had most likely suffered violence at home. The journalist, after a few moments of silence, replied, 'Yes, you are right, that is me.'

These women are there for other women; taking the lead, reporting upon the need to protect all of them, excluding none of them. Dame Nemat Shafik, former director of the International Monetary Fund and, until recently, deputy governor of the Bank of England, is another example. Her appointment at the Bank of England is a peculiar fact if we consider that 90 per cent of top jobs in finance are taken by high-achieving men. Finance should be taught to boys and girls from an early age. It should be included in the primary school curriculum. Women holding top positions represent a minority, so the election of a woman governor is still a great event. As was the appointment of Marisa Drew as co-head of global markets at Credit Suisse. She was recently named one of the seventeen most influential women in the world of global finance. She declared that having more women at the top of finance would help not only women but also finance itself, since diversity almost always brings a considerable improvement in results.

Research carried out by Credit Suisse looking at 3,000 companies has, in fact, highlighted that companies run by boards of directors which include women record greater profits and have higher performance standards, together with stronger growth rates. Another survey led by McKinsey and Catalyst underlines how, in an employment sector, a minority group needs the help of affirmative action at the beginning to achieve independence later. Such help can be limited in time, since the minority stops needing external assistance once a certain power level has been reached. The level at which affirmative action is no longer required has been measured at 30 per cent. It means that as long as the presence of women is below 30 per cent, action is needed in order to increase the number of women in certain fields and eventually reach a fair representation in the workplace. As we know, the key sectors are politics, finance and the economy. In the UK in 2016, the major banks adopted a Chart of Intents, listing a number of voluntary proposals aimed at increasing women's presence in the workplace, improving their working life and stimulating their professional growth. The main points of the chart recommend:

- appointing an executive in charge of gender, diversity and inclusion
- establishing internal objectives for gender equality within top management
- publishing gender statistics on the participating banks' websites each year
- linking senior executives' salary with the achievement of the objectives

Sharing the chart has been made possible thanks to the intervention of women politicians and top finance women. Among them was Harriett Baldwin, who played a key role. The former economic secretary to the treasury observed that financial services are the best-paid sectors, but that they also have the highest gender pay gap: 39.5

per cent compared to 19.2 per cent in the other economic sectors.

Another key woman is Jayne-Anne Gadhia, head of Virgin Money. She reports what has already been highlighted by Credit Suisse; that the average return on capital for companies with just one woman is 16 per cent in comparison to 12 per cent for companies deprived of female representation. Increasing women's involvement would add 600 billion pounds to the UK economy, and by 2030 the British economy would see a 10 per cent rise.

According to Marisa Drew, women bring a different perspective to the decision-making process, since they look at risks in a different way. So, we need their points of view if we want to enhance our financial system. Marisa advises young women who enter the finance world, encouraging them to be passionate about their jobs: she says that only a strong passion leads to success. Self-confidence, awareness and attitude make the difference, she believes. And, she adds, never be afraid to ask! She manages roughly 750 people, many of whom often knock at her door to ask for special tasks, salary increases or career advancement. How many women are among them? None. Her main piece of advice for women who have already become successful in finance is to leave their comfort zone and take risks if they want to reach the top. That is what she did and her boldness led her to achieve her greatest successes.

It is important to have a life out of the office as well; it is essential to have hobbies, a family, other issues to argue about. Women should not become like men. Femininity and sensitivity are added value, not handicaps. When women are fully focused on their work and have positions of responsibility, they find the time and strength to fulfil their other obligations. It is part of us, it is a sort of innate motherhood that motivates us to uphold great ideals.

Amal Alamuddin is among the best-known civil-rights lawyers. She is the epitome of a successful woman who devotes herself to high causes. She became famous because she is George Clooney's wife but she was already internationally renowned for her degree of commitment and the battles she has waged on behalf of international human rights. Her husband provided a great example to other men as well by marrying her and supporting her publicly. Clooney could have chosen a young model, with no battles to fight. But he was not afraid of loving a redoubtable woman who had built her career upon her skills, ideals, humanity and courage.

Shadow Attorney General for England and Wales Shami Chakrabarti is another woman making England, and the entire world, shine because of her commitment and what she represents. She was the director of Liberty, a group defending human rights, from 2003 to 2016. She is considered by many to be the most influential Asian woman in Britain. Lady Chakrabarti argues that according to data, austerity is primarily a female issue. She declared that women are far more affected by budget cuts than men. They are more likely to be single parents, to earn less or to work part-time than their male counterparts, leaving them far more reliant on the state. Non-white women are then three times disadvantaged: on grounds of gender, ethnic group and salary. This is why she claims that the government should stop cutting the budget indiscriminately, and instead start implementing policies of social support, beginning with those addressing gender inequality and giving priority to the support of women in difficult positions. Gender budgeting is good budgeting.

The golden list could go on and on and it should provide hope, courage and power, especially to those who live in a cage and cannot see a way out in their lifetime. They are trapped on diminishing professional and personal paths, living in countries which do not support women's emancipation. They still have to build their identity as women but they must not give up; the examples of others will give them hope and help them fight.

Barbara Stocking is a leader among activists. Former head of Oxfam International, the NGO with the biggest international network, operating in more than a hundred countries, she is currently president of Murray Edwards College. In 2010, the *Financial Times* asked her for her 'golden rule'. She simply replied that it was to give the same value to all of us, explaining that she does not change her behaviour whether with her shopkeeper or with the Secretary-General of the United Nations, as they are both human beings.

This is why I say that women are 'saving the world'; it is because they have an attitude of love towards the world. They own an empathetic and multifaceted perspective, not only a self-centred one. Women's contribution in terms of sensitivity and creativity is essential in all sectors, especially in artistic ones. With their own ability to sense the invisible and make it visible, creative women influence customs and fashion, shaping a new sense of beauty no longer centred on male ideals. Let us consider Stella McCartney; Paul's daughter, a successful fashion designer who became an entrepreneur and took on new challenges, making a career which owed nothing to her father. And then Phoebe Philo, with her thin body and imposing genius, who turned the Chloé brand inside out, leading it for five years and changing the line into one of the most innovative and successful on the market. At the peak of her success she unexpectedly made an even braver decision: she retired to devote herself to her family. It was time for her to put her personal life and her children first. Two years later, she was back on the world stage, becoming director of Céline after Bernard Arnault, the president of LVMH, asked her to lead the brand. Once again, she performed a miracle: she channeled the renewed energy from her 'love break' into relaunching and revitalising the line.

This is an example of what being a woman means: it means being multidimensional. Like Emma Watson, who was once a little witch and then turned into an activist. As a witness to women's courage from a young age, she decided to support women's rights by speaking out in the United Nations' campaign HeForShe. Hermione, the heroine of the *Harry Potter* saga, a great role model, has chosen a task more difficult than any of those in her adventures: she takes advantage of her power and visibility to provide inspiration; she takes it upon herself to become a gender role model. Thanks to Emma, the girls of her generation, usually inspired by totally different icons, can open their eyes and ponder important issues. Because of brave women like her, who are prepared to step up to the plate and show their courage and sensitivity, England can start a global surge of awareness.

We have seen Kate Winslet playing widely celebrated roles which have brought her more than one Academy Award nomination. But more than anything, right from the start, we admired her for opposing a system which favoured appearance over substance; for standing out against the plastic world into which we all, men and women, are plunged without even noticing it. A world that uses plastic surgery and Photoshop editing software to change our features, instead of delighting in the uniqueness of our imperfect faces and the tokens of our age. Kate stays the same – she has not aligned herself with 6-8 standard sizes – and she has gone further. Going all the way back to the days of *Titanic*, she has prioritised the importance of her feelings. She has chosen not to neglect her family and personal life in pursuit of success and public recognition. She did not attend the preview of the film, which would have endeared her to Hollywood, because it was on the day of her first fiancé Stephen Tredre's funeral. He died of cancer at the age of 34. Winslet confessed that she felt a great sadness. All that remained was their closeness until the end. She would have loved him always. He had been part of her life since she was fifteen. Together with the purity of her feelings goes a firm belief in honesty; she defended and still defends the right to put on weight during pregnancy and welcomes a few extra kilos. She replies to critics that one should try never to cast doubts on oneself. And she advises girls to carry on and face their fears and insecurities. She knows her mind and wants to feel good about herself the way she is.

This is another way to fight for all women, especially when some are such slaves to their appearance that they make themselves ill trying to conform to a predefined body shape. The aim of true feminism is to set you free from the chains of stereotypes. Set you free from the sense of inadequacy. Set you free from the fear of not pleasing. Being set free also means learning to say no:

we have been educated to please men for centuries, to take care of them and the family before taking care of ourselves; to accept being victims and not complain. We have been taught to be modest, pleasing, tame; to give up our pleasure for the benefit of others. Yet it is not wrong for us to reject doing something we do not want to do. Learning to say no is liberating; personal agency is the key to emancipation.

In England, wherever I look I see important and well-known women sending messages to inspire all their sisters with courage. Here I quote a small extract from Helen Mirren's beautiful speech on the importance of being a feminist:

No matter what sex you are, or race, be a feminist. In every country and culture that I have visited, from Sweden to Uganda, from Singapore to Mali, it is clear that when women are given respect, and the ability and freedom to pursue their personal dreams and ambitions, life improves for everyone. I didn't define myself as a feminist until quite recently, but I had always lived like a feminist and believed in the obvious: that women were as capable and as energetic and as inspiring as men. But to join a movement called feminism seemed too didactic, too political. However, I have come to understand that feminism is not an abstract idea but a necessity if we – and really by 'we', I mean you guys – are to move us forward and not backward into ignorance and fearful jealousy. So now I am a declared feminist and I would encourage you to be the same.

In *The Little Prince*, Antoine de Saint-Exupéry maintained that the essential was often invisible to the eyes; well now it has become clearly visible to us all. We are ready; we are protagonists in all fields, from politics to the arts. This is a wake-up call to all of us who are free to decide about our own existence – from the book we want to read, to the dress we wish to wear. But it is mostly directed at those who are not insisting on their own fundamental rights. Threats, abandonment, tyranny and violence – too many crimes will continue to be committed in the world until we finally achieve gender equality.

The example of these well-known British women proves that it is possible to overcome gender bias by sheer strength of personality and arrive at equality with one's dignity intact. Aphra Behn was the first one to do that: 'for bread,' she used to say, shifting the attention from her gender to her struggle for the right to work. With a queen's dignity and a warrior's courage, she condemned the social customs of her time, using the only weapons she had: courage and talent. She was not happy just with writing. She dared to make human rights and women's plight her main issues, instead of romantic love. Knowing the position of many women at the end of the seventeenth century, the era in which she lived, she was aware she was privileged. She chose to use her position to fight against discrimination and to promote freedom as well as equality, but she paid the heavy price of injustice, which cost more than the 500 pounds she used to earn each month. She was held captive inside the cage of moralism, but she knew that since she could support herself with her own money, she could afford to take risks. And she endured two periods of imprisonment. I am convinced that this extraordinary woman was the mother of feminism, a precarious movement even four centuries later. An *ante litteram* feminist and everlasting genius, she was a woman like all others in her feelings, like few in her intellect and like none in the literature of her times.

When I think about how many women I need to thank sincerely, I lose count. So many Amazons of our evolution, using not physical but inner strength, have saved the world, or at least a piece of it, thus proving to be pioneering agents of change.

Thanks to some of them I can now cast my vote, since before the struggle for universal suffrage I was not even considered able to decide who could represent me. I was part of a subcategory. I did not own any rights, but men had rights they could exercise over me. Mine is an extremely painful story of submission, hatred and violence, starting thousands of years ago and still far from over. Even today I get beaten for saying more than one word. At the same time, on the other side of the world, I get crowned with laurel because of my brilliant mind. Great souls, personalities beyond time flying with wings of courage and freedom, intrepid women burst through the chains prepared for them before they were born. Meanwhile, we keep fighting against infibulation; it is still considered regrettable for a woman to experience pleasure. We are humiliated right from the start; beaten even before we have the chance to fight. That is why we need stars of such brightness and intensity to keep shining and lighting the way for others.

Another remarkable woman is anthropologist Jane Goodall, director and founder of the Jane Goodall Institute which concerns itself with the protection of primates worldwide. With a degree in biology and qualifications in ethology and anthropology, in 1957 she went to Kenya to carry out research on chimpanzees. After fifty years, she is still fighting to safeguard the environment and animal rights. Her institute has dozens of branches in several countries and is dedicated to the development of Africa. Jane is eighty-two and she still has a battle to fight, the most difficult one: saving not only the animals on the planet but the planet itself. On the occasion of the Congress of the International Union for the Conservation of Nature in Honolulu, she declared, 'I do have hope for the future, even though I think I have seen as much as anybody of the harm that we are inflicting on this planet.' She revealed that she draws strength from young people thanks to the Roots and Shoots programme which, since 1991, has spread awareness of the need to teach children respect for people, animals and the environment.

Each of the women I have talked about works tirelessly to benefit the whole human community. They all believe in achieving great ideals and actively battle against poverty and inequality. They are successful women with international reputations, besides being mothers and wives. That is what the women of the world are today, and England's are the first in line.

I would like to conclude with a rather less high-profile woman. She is a British hermit nun, a role model not only for the men and women of her time, but for the Church, too. She is the daughter of J.R. Glorney Bolton, a writer on Gandhi as well as Pope John XXIII's biographer. She was born an Anglican but converted to Catholicism. She became a translator, calligrapher, poet, university lecturer, nun, hermit and philanthropist in addition to being a wife and mother of four children. Today she fights on behalf of ethnic minorities and takes care of the English Cemetery in Florence, a holy, cultural and prestigious place where the major British poets and illustrious personalities who died in Italy were buried. The cemetery was assigned to her care by the Swiss Reformed Church.

Julia Bolton is devoted to faith and truth and leads a life of severe self-discipline. But she cannot stop working for others, as well. Julia commits herself to those who are in need, in spite of the fact that she is more than eighty-three years old and has already fought many battles. Her current focus is the serious problem presented by the Romani communities in Italy, who live by stealing and cause social disorder in dangerous and degrading camps. Among them, there are women and unprotected children. Everything started one evening when Sister Julia met, by chance, a young Romani mother who had just given birth. The woman was breastfeeding on the steps of a church during a heavy storm and the nun decided to take her to her convent. For a few years now, Bolton has welcomed the Romani into her cemetery, turning it into a library and a place of culture with a guest house for emergencies. She was brave enough to ask for cemetery renovation work to be entrusted to the Romani, who have finely restored the ancient and often precious gravestones. She told me of her belief in them. She saw that most Romani women are skilful artisans: clean, careful and respectful. They love Diderot and Alembert's encyclopedia. She argued that they have an incredible craving for culture. Later, Sister Julia talked to me about Romani women again. She was firmly convinced that even the last among the least can be supportive and can help fight for women's rights. As a consequence of this conversation, an international project arose supporting Romani women artisans in building cradles for the luckier next generation of children.

No identity

We can lose ourselves in many ways, but most of the time we are lost because we have never found ourselves in the first place.

Teenagers have always found it difficult to identify themselves, and this is the case even more today, when the image is easily distorted by vanity and the craving for popularity at any price. Facebook and Instagram have replaced not only books but the possibility to meet and self-promote ourselves as we really are. In some parts of the world, one goes naked in front of strangers, enhanced by Photoshop, while, at the other extreme, women are forced to wear headscarves because of traditions supported by law in the name of religion.

The all-enveloping veil covering many Arab women from head to toe, leaving only the eyes visible, is a symbol of enslavement. Especially when we see these black shadows walking among the people of a modern city like London. Under the pretext of multiculturalism and respect for religion, we have lost sight of women's right to human dignity. The Koran does not say that women have to cover themselves head to toe; it is a tradition invented by men. And traditions can either be handed down or can cease to exist. How much do economic and political interests affect the indifference in the media and in our culture at large? Do we shut our eyes to women's rights in the name of money and power?

The United Kingdom is a place of safety. Such a civilised and enlightened country, ruled by an ancient and respectful democracy, must protect these women, even when it comes to the way they dress. Abayas, niqabs and burqas can be seen on Buckingham Palace Road or in Hyde Park, and are even worn by very young women – as far as we can guess just by looking at their eyes. They are accompanied by men wearing Western-style clothes and even jeans and T-shirts in hot weather – they can please themselves! They may be their fathers, husbands, brothers; certainly guardians of some sort. Each time I look at this scene I feel pity for these women and contempt for the bold men walking by their side. How can a man, apparently a modern one, living in a country where women's freedom is an everyday fact of life, not pause to ponder? Does he not empathise with the woman he presumably loves? Does he not reflect on her physical discomfort, when they walk together in the sun? Does he not think that she would like to mix with other women and adapt to local ways of dressing, the same way he does? To be covered is to be deprived of individuality and freedom. A black shadow with no identity. My impression is that the only one gaining their rights is always and only him; the man walking in pride, as if he were showing off his caught prey. He can do everything, even deprive her of her own identity.

Traditions must evolve. I wonder about a role reversal; I wonder about how men would feel walking in a crowd covered from head to toe. It would take them just one day to understand what it means to live like a ghost. Anyway, no woman would think of wrapping up her partner. Women do not need to feel that sense of ownership. Women have never fabricated traditions damaging men's rights. Let us remember that, please. I wish that Muslim men living in the UK would reflect on the current legitimacy of such outmoded customs.

It is interesting to note that this problem does not arise for the very lucky and rich female Saudi royals attending private clubs in London and wearing elegant Western clothes. I hope their example helps the women less fortunate to enjoy the same freedom, both in the UK and in their own countries.

We face a serious problem in that we have got used to all of this. We have lost our ability to become indignant about it. Nobel Peace Prize winner Elie Wiesel's speech on the dangers of indifference, in reference to the Nazis' persecution of the Jews, seems relevant. German citizens at that time stood by and let it happen, without getting angry, without feeling pity, unmoved by the victims' suffering. In his beautiful speech, Wiesel talked about the essence of this attitude and the threat it poses to a community:

> Of course, indifference can be tempting – more than that, seductive. It is so much easier to look away from victims. It is so much easier to avoid such rude interruptions to our work, our dreams, our hopes. It is, after all, awkward, troublesome, to be involved in another person's pain and despair. Yet, for the person who is indifferent, his or her neighbours are of no consequence. And, therefore, their lives are meaningless. Their hidden or even visible anguish is of no interest. Indifference reduces the other to an abstraction... Indifference, after all, is more dangerous than anger and hatred.

This is why we should all pay attention to the violation of women's dignity, to the moral framework that enslaves them as well as their physical incarceration. Behind the black curtain, most of the time there is a possessive husband who thinks it his duty to ensure that his wife respects tradition and covers herself to avoid the attraction of other men and the threat of their unchecked desire.

This is totally wrong, as women are not objects to be controlled and covered and if the lust of other men does in fact pose a threat, we might think to start there rather than by restricting the freedoms of women!

Very often women are well supported economically by their husbands, and accept dependent conditions in exchange for a luxury lifestyle. But to deny our own identity is an insult to life itself, which provided us with specific and unique features. Our faces and bodies are precious indicators for our entire beings. What opinion of women will the son of a wholly veiled mother form? How will he behave with his partner, once an adult? I wonder about this and hope that a global debate will be set off from England. Religious freedom must not become an excuse for denying women their rights. All religions must be safeguarded and respected. But so must all women. Nothing and no one can restrict our rights, not even God. He/She indisputably supports our well-being and our achievement.

Where do the boundaries lie between religion, superstition and the cultural traditions often invented and passed on by men without the input of women? In Germany, a good code of practice has been introduced. It could be applied in the UK as well. I am talking about the liberal set of rules which govern the new mosque founded by Turkish lawyer Mrs Seyran Ateş, who explains the peculiarity of the place: 'Fundamentally, the mosque's door is open for everyone, men and women, heterosexuals and gay men, Sunnis, Shia and non-Muslims. With one exception: No one will come in with a niqab or burqa.' This is the future. It is not by chance that it was a woman that had this great idea. She herself declared that the all-enveloping veil has nothing to do with religion.

Rich and poor, Western and Arab, we all suffer from men's bad decisions because of the power and influence they have over our lives. In Western countries, many of us are slaves without even knowing it. Without even realising it we are governed by extremely dangerous conditioning. We have been exposed our whole lives to an ideal of female perfection, represented by ethereal, unreal figures; skinny but with exaggerated breasts and bottoms, the body parts that catch men's attention most. Men rule not only the religious sphere but also the secular, the mundane. Major fashion brands' designers are almost always men. They foster an image of a 'perfect' woman that is halfway between a plastic doll and a terminally ill patient. She is spindly, with sunken eyes and prominent cheekbones; with either no breasts or bottom, or unnaturally huge ones, always on a skinny body. This is an unreal image, an emblem of an abstract and distorted view of female identity.

Plastic surgeons from across the world are now reporting an alarming new phenomenon: 13- to 18-year-old girls resorting to plastic surgery. They want to change their breasts, lips, noses, cheekbones, hips, legs, even buttocks. They are supported and accompanied along this painful and dangerous path by their own mothers who underwent the same interventions. Why? Because they are unhappy with their own bodies and want to look like popular icons of beauty, without realising that it is impossible to emulate what does not exist. The outcome is that we all become homogenous and eternally dissatisfied. A perverse mechanism drives our misguided struggle to please a system aimed at destroying our identity. We embrace what is just another way to enslave us.

Teenagers are obsessed with diet, often fasting or abstaining from certain foods. Anorexia and bulimia have become a social scourge. We get sick when we are very young as we have to be slim at all costs. And we keep feeling inadequate as adults as well, resorting to toxic, often lethal, diets, and to surgery which sometimes disfigures us. A woman's life is dominated by a fight against nature involving Botox, acids, injections, lifting and blepharoplasty. We forget beauty is subjective; it is a random harmony of shapes, not a pre-printed model. We are sold a mistaken perception of our own body, which affects adversely our whole world of feelings and relationships. Who said skinny is beautiful? On the contrary, healthy is beautiful. Strong is beautiful. We should all eat healthy food and do regular physical exercise: these are essential lifestyle choices.

Sport can help young women to feel strong and comfortable in their own bodies. I love martial arts and regret not having practised them when I was a child. At that time, girls could either do dancing or rhythmic gymnastics. Had I practised kick boxing, karate or kung fu, I would have enjoyed exercise more. Such disciplines are still uncommon among women, but should become common practice, together with krav maga, if only for the purpose of self-defence against the constant threats we face, inside and outside the home.

The most erroneous message influencing the social imagination of the young, and of adults too, is that a woman cannot simply be the way she is. The film industry contributes to all this, especially through its attitude to ageing. Though old and grizzled, with marked wrinkles and sagging skin, men perform sex-symbol roles. Their physical abilities are highlighted, they perform action scenes and go through overwhelming passions on the set as well as in real life. Robert Redford and Sean Connery embody male beauty standards in that their age is an attractive, or insignificant, quality. Women, when they perform roles in their old age, play only mature roles. By the time they are thirty they are considered old by the fashion and film industries. There is no such thing as eternal youth, silicone or no silicone.

The issue is so serious as to require government measures. Thanks to a woman minister, France is among the first countries to put a stop to the glorification of thinness and preternaturally perfect shapes. This is why we need more women in government; to draw attention to certain issues, change the dominant culture and improve our daily lives. In the interests of women's physical and psychological health, on 3 April 2015 France approved an amendment to its reform of the health system preventing underweight girls from walking the catwalk. They also passed another decree forbidding the glorification of thinness and banning websites which encourage anorexia. In 2016, the Parliament voted to compel magazines and advertising posters to specify whether pictures have been retouched. Extreme measures were necessary to get back to reality: a reality we run away from because of the fear of growing old, putting on weight, not pleasing. Chasing illusory perfection to comply with body-image trends can often lead to relationship problems and an incapacity to love others – but most of all, an incapacity to love ourselves.

The majority of surgical interventions, particularly in the case of models, concern sucking fat from the inner thighs and injecting it into the buttocks. That many beautiful and very young women are insecure enough to undergo such crazy interventions is very disturbing. Beauty is currently measured according to the gap between the legs and the shape of the buttocks. Adult women, of course, want to appear younger at all costs. Hence, they undergo a series of procedures to remedy everything right down to their facial expressions. Chinese girls increasingly resort to plastic surgery to look like Europeans. They totally undervalue themselves. This is a plastic world that is making us sicker and weaker. We are creating something destined not to bear fruit; a sterile society. We should hardly be surprised if our misguided 'therapies' cause unhappiness and frustration. We cannot pander to the obsessions of celebrities, who are often fragile people with inner troubles. We have to encourage individuality, strength, concrete ideas, and provide girls with different role models.

Women can become their own fiercest enemies, rising up against those who do not comply with the same canons of beauty. If you have cellulite, a crooked nose, wide hips, you are not up to it. So we turn on each other and fight amongst ourselves. Today, a woman's aim should not be to snatch up the best husband, as has been her law of survival over the centuries. Today our aim should not be to become the most desirable, at the cost of turning into inflatable dolls with no wrinkles. We are just humiliating ourselves as well as losing our individuality.

I got rid of such conditioning only when I was in my late thirties. Up to then, I used to be a slave, like almost all of us. Because you cannot help it. Social pressure is crushing. You have need of a more powerful strength of spirit than those who influence fashion and customs, those who create culture; often misogynists, male-chauvinist men, or women who are even more chauvinist than them without even realising it. You live in a crystal nightmare, you are a puppet of your own free will. You have to be slimmer, younger: aims that are unhealthy and incompatible with a harmonious life. It does not matter how much you have already accomplished. You could have studied, started companies, had children, but if you do not look like the stereotype, you do not feel desirable. In order to get rid of such obsessions, you must fly higher than the crowd, break through the wall of misguided beliefs that have been leading you to compete against your own nature. You cannot change the rules on your own, but you can refuse to play the game. In this way, you will become your own person.

Many women, though beautiful and successful, in possession of many virtues and skills, do not reveal their age. As if it were something to be ashamed of. On the contrary, we should be proud of our age; the length of time we have been on this earth has allowed us to grow our talent and helped us to look the way we look. A man with wrinkles may be sexy; the same should be said of a woman. I see too many women censuring themselves. Now that I'm finally in my forties, I can say that it is wonderful. I would never go back to my twenties. So-called 'beauty' is a waste of time, money and energy. Michelle Obama is right when she advises girls to spend less time making themselves beautiful and more time studying maths. We become women against women when we are very young, without realising that it is men who are creating this sense of competition among us.

The secret is to love yourself and let others love the way you are; to love yourself as a person and as a woman, regardless of men. I have managed to change not only myself, but also many men over the years. I opened my world to them, what I had discovered and achieved by leaving some marshy lands: conditioning areas. Luckily, real men, the clever and self-confident ones, appreciate those who face them with reality: self-confident women. Those who truly love themselves the way they are.

'Do not be afraid,' said Pope John Paul II, then Benedict XVI and finally Pope Francis, quoting the Gospel, to encourage the young most of all. Because fear paralyses society; in particular the fear of not pleasing, caused by a loss of self-confidence. If you had never seen yourself in a mirror with your own eyes, you would not know what you really looked like. You must have faith, faith in yourself. And if someone is not able to appreciate you, it is their own problem. There are intelligent men who can see beyond outward appearances; men who are not attracted to plastic and 'perfect' shapes. You meet them when you start looking for communion with another soul, after having achieved it with your own.

Seek out those who respect your ideals. Have the courage to leave behind those who make you feel imperfect. Your aim is to be authentic, not perfect. Those who do not accept your specific features are beneath you. Such freedom from judgement also applies if you are looking for the love of another woman. The lesbian community in the UK is more powerful than in Italy and provides many great examples of women overcoming prejudice to live fulfilling, emancipated lives. They fully understand what it means to get rid of stereotypes but, unfortunately, even here lesbians continue to face many difficulties. Within the LGBT world, lesbians are still the least visible ones.

My friends Shamim Sarif and Hanan Kattan are leading a great battle against stereotypes and discrimination. They are respectively a Muslim Indian and a Christian Palestinian, adopted by London, happily married and the mothers of two wonderful boys. They are authors, film directors and producers of masterpieces where the issues of sexual, social and racial difference, as well as discrimination, are always addressed with deep sensitivity and intelligence. I particularly loved one of their first movies, *I Can't Think Straight*, based on Shamim's book, which tells the romantic story of two gorgeous girls who come from different religious, social and cultural backgrounds. The film is witty, fun and enlightened, despite the intensity of the misogyny and homophobia that the protagonists are forced to confront on account of their families' attitudes; in particular those of one of their mothers. This story happens to not only be real but that of their own relationship and struggle for personal happiness. I find it amazing that, not only have they bravely fought their own families' misguided disapprobation and the endemic prejudice in society to build a beautiful relationship and fulfilling lives, but they've also written a book and produced a film based on this story to inspire lesbian girls around the world and reassure them that, despite everything, you can always win: love wins. Shamim and Hanan know that common sense, culture and empathy are the keys to understanding yourself and others. Accepting others comes with accepting yourself and your fears. Again, here are examples of free and successful women who keep fighting for a better world and inspiring other women. They are part of the silent army which is marching and already saving the world. We need their view of the world and we need more women film directors as well as producers to make us see life through their lens.

Meanwhile, other women keep educating their girls in the traditional way, which is to say in a way calculated to preserve the patriarchal society. They look backwards, thinking that it is safer to live in the shadow of dominant characters; they are unable to imagine a society which is different from the one they were born in. They believe in having a 'strongman' who can lead you in the family as well as in politics. President Trump is an example of a 'strongman'; he belongs to the past in terms of women's issues and yet he was voted in by many conservative women as he reflects their own ideology. He is also supported by women who love such macho archetypes that push the very limits of misogyny; they are geisha, used to serving; victims, used to suffering; alienated women who do not understand the harm of certain behaviours, who do not question themselves, who are indifferent. Despite them, the patriarchal society will come to an end; in some places sooner than in others, but it will come to an end. It may take hundreds of years, but women's freedom will win. A stronger, more fervid wish for emancipation will gain ground. The seed will grow, germinate. It will be spread by communication, it will reach all countries. This will happen.

What we can all do today is try to open the eyes of the majority of the people we meet; men and women. Let us practise empathy, the most necessary emotion. Let us wear the clothes of those who suffer oppression. The grip of hatred, war and unconditional power crushes us. The grip has been tightened by male governments over the centuries. But even if the grip is rocklike, a rock cannot stem the tide. Women are a river bursting its banks. Haters, misogynists and those who practise discrimination cannot stop us.

If you are a man, close your eyes for a few minutes and take a deep breath; see yourself in a woman's body, a young girl who has suffered violence, who has been discriminated against, who does not have opportunities in life, who could not study, who has had to marry too early, who has no contact with the world away from the domestic hearth. Try to identify with her, to feel what she feels. It should be a daily exercise to increase your understanding that we all need to do something to support women. By taking care of her, of this young girl, you will help yourself as well, your children, the children of your children, since you will be fighting for a better society. A fairer society.

The 'strongman' is he who defends and appreciates women when they smile and nod but who despises and stops considering them when they reveal their own personality. In the last few years, along with women's emancipation, we have seen powerful political leaders taking high office across the world. Leaders who regularly betray their own wives, tolerate women's commercialisation and exercise a political dominance that is inherently sexist: they range from Bill Clinton, former president of the United States, to François Hollande, former president of the French Republic; from Arnold Schwarzenegger, former Governor of California, to Silvio Berlusconi, former prime minister of the Italian Republic. In Italy I was disgusted to witness the total disregard for women's dignity by former Prime Minister Berlusconi during his time in office. Now he is old – a grandfather – but he used to surround himself with very young girls, often minors, to satisfy his animal instincts, using precious energy to organise parties, dubbed '*bunga bunga*' by the media, instead of devoting himself to the selfless service of the nation the electorate should expect. My indignation is also directed at the girls, who clearly sold their own bodies hoping for a reward in terms of houses, cars or appearances on TV. This is surely the most hateful sort of prostitution. The emptiness and greed of women who 'stay afloat' through the pursuit of rich men's money and hope to gain popularity by appearing on reality shows seem to know no bounds. Some of them, after the Italian scandal and the ruin of their 'reputations', moved to London, where they live behind fake identities cynically fleecing old, rich and powerful men. Reality is stranger than fiction.

The scandals of Deputy Weiner, caught sending sad sexual self-portraits to young girls, and Democratic Senator John Edwards, guilty of having lied about his adultery and his illegitimate child, add two more names to the list of powerful men holding public office who do not respect the first and most important institution: family. Already on the list is the bigamous President François Mitterrand, who is officially married to Danielle, the mother of his children, yet also has a second family and lots of lovers. Years go by but the scandals keep on emerging. President François Hollande was the subject of tabloid headlines because of his affair with actress Julie Gayet. The pictures published by the weekly paper *Closer* show the president arriving at the woman's house by scooter, on the morning of one New Year's Eve, followed by a bodyguard carrying croissants. Bill Clinton is a paradigm of such adulterous political leaders who conduct their private lives in a way that makes them unfit for public office. Since 1978, three years after his marriage to Hillary Clinton, his path has been strewn with accusations of sexual harassment, quite apart from the well-known 'sex-gate' scandal of 1995 involving Monica Lewinsky. If such male role models are not brought to account, women in the West have only themselves to blame. We can't tolerate this any longer.

How important is economic self-sufficiency in the process of asserting our ideas and building our self-respect? Economic self-sufficiency is definitely women's surest path to the achievement of high self-esteem and the discovery of their own value; it is dependency that enslaves them. If we can choose what to do, where and how to live, whether to save or spend money and on what to spend that money for ourselves and for our children, we will feel a greater freedom to think and judge, as well. We will be free to reject, for the sake of survival, male chauvinism and insulting behaviours. We will be free to choose who rules us, as well. Up to now, our choices, including political ones, have been imposed on us by a subtle slavery which we cannot get to grips with.

Britain's highly evolved legal system ensures respect for women and their rights. It does not sanction the election of political representatives who promote chauvinistic male behaviours. Thanks to the election of a young, enlightened, forward-looking president, with more than one university degree, and with an unprejudiced idea of love – so much so that he married an older woman instead of a young ex-model – France is changing too. Simone Veil is to be interred in the Panthéon of Paris, together with the great men of France. A woman magistrate, member of the Constitutional Council and the first president of the European Parliament, she, as a minister, supported the introduction of the 1974 law on abortion in France. The decision that she will rest in the Panthéon was taken thanks to Macron: a signal that he means to favour women's issues, and a tribute to the sublime personality of Veil, who is only the fifth woman to be accorded the privilege.

The unwritten law is always the same: to be worth as much as a man you must fly so high as not to be equalled, not only by men, but also by other women. When the women of the whole world can study and work, when they are independent and have inner strength, then there will be no 'strongmen' elected to form governments that embody human frailty. Then the dominant societal archetype, patriarchy, that has led the earth to environmental collapse and produced so many wars and social discrepancies, will come to an end. Then highly evolved women will have gained power and will be able to implement more equal laws and devote their efforts to healing the world and setting men and women free from ignorance and slavery. And the values women cherish will prevail: cooperation, acceptance, equality, justice, care, sharing, inclusion, love. We will choose peace instead of war. We will look at long-term development, instead of short-term growth. We will care for the community, instead of for a small elite.

I am sure all this will happen. The Dalai Lama, talking at the Vancouver Summit for Peace in 2009, in the presence of Nobel Peace Prize winners Mairead Maguire, Betty Williams and Jody Williams, said that, 'The world will be saved by Western women.' I prefer believing that it will be saved by all women, whatever nationality, colour or religion: united and resolute at last.

6
2017: A Year of Change

'Unlike the laws of physics, which are free of
inconsistencies, every man-made order is packed
with internal contradictions. Cultures are
constantly trying to reconcile these contradictions,
and this process fuels change.'

Yuval Noah Harari

2017 has not been a 'business as usual' year for women
around the world. It has indeed been a year of women's
liberation and we now expect nothing less from the
years to come. Merriam-Webster, America's most-trusted
online dictionary, declared 'feminism' the 'Word of the
Year'. It is no surprise that feminism – defined as 'the
theory of the political, economic, and social equality of
the sexes' and 'organized activity on behalf of women's
rights and interests' – was this year's most searched
word: following the #MeToo campaign, a viral sensation
arising from the abhorrent Weinstein scandal, in 2017
thousands of women finally found the courage to speak
out against the sexual harassment and abuses they had
faced. At last, after centuries of silence, a despicable
pattern of behaviour has become insufferable in the eyes
of society. Urged by the American actress Alyssa Milano
to share their stories via the #MeToo Twitter hashtag,
thousands of women responded. At its peak, the hashtag
was tweeted half a million times in twenty-four hours
alone.

Harvey Weinstein, a Hollywood film mogul, was accused by Ronan Farrow in an article for the *New York Times* of sexually harassing actresses and even now the repercussions of these allegations show no sign of abating. Weinstein faces the break-up of his business empire and police investigations in both the US and UK after dozens of actresses and assistants came forward to make allegations of rape and sexual abuse. Many of the victims told of how he had demanded naked massages, exposed himself without their consent or lunged at them. They all described a man who would readily and ruthlessly use his power to control them; use the threat of damaging their careers to blackmail them into submission. His accusers have given women a voice worldwide. They are no longer afraid to condemn the actions of powerful men. Apparently everyone in Hollywood knew about him and his bad behaviour, even though no one had the courage to talk before 2017. This must make us pause to consider the oppressive nature of a culture that admits bad behaviour, especially when those given free rein already have a very tangible source of power.

'Abusers create an environment where you feel incredibly isolated, and that if you tell anyone there will be consequences; or your shame about what's happened means that you keep it to yourself. Realising you're not alone is a very powerful thing,' said Sarah Champion, the former shadow minister for women and equalities in the UK and a longstanding campaigner against sexual abuse. The problem of violence against women, both psychological and physical, is a very serious matter, a social emergency that our governments still don't address with the required strength and determination. In a major study, published last year in the UK by the TUC and campaign group Everyday Sexism, half of the women surveyed said they had been sexually harassed at work, rising to almost two-thirds of women under 24, though most of them did not make formal complaints. More shockingly, research from Girlguiding UK found nearly two-thirds of girls aged over 13 had been sexually harassed at school, with behaviour ranging from taunts and jokes to groping.

'Sexual harassment does bring shame. And I think it's really powerful that this transfer is happening, that these women are able not just to share their shame but to put the shame where it belongs: on the perpetrator.' I strongly agree with these words from Tarana Burke, the African-American woman who created the 'Me too' campaign in 2006 to encourage women to show solidarity with one another, a movement that went viral only in 2017 after it was relaunched by Alyssa Milano using a Twitter hashtag. It took a whole eleven years and a deplorable Hollywood scandal such as the Weinstein affair to get the publicity it deserved. This dynamic demonstrates just how difficult it is for women to free themselves from the chains of silence and indifference. The problem is that for centuries society was built to encourage such silence and submission: men, especially powerful men, could harass you without shame, without taking any responsibility, while safe in the knowledge that their status and the dominant patriarchal culture protected them, that the fear of their victims prevented their crimes from being divulged. Historically, sexual assaulters have protected themselves by inducing shame in their victims. This, finally, is ending: #MeToo is a revolutionary movement that will change society for ever. Of course, women should not take advantage of their new powers; pretending they have been harassed or abused. This is now the fear of many men, but I'm sure that cases of such deception will be few and far between and insignificant in the face of the momentous and wonderful change that we are now seeing: women have found the courage to talk and men are finally scared of the potential for shameful public exposure if they harass women.

In 2017, for the first time in its history, *Time* gave its prestigious 'Person of the Year' nomination to more than just one person; in its December issue it paid tribute to all 'The Silence Breakers', 'the voices that launched a movement', with a cover featuring five of the most influential champions of the #MeToo cause. This is an incredible recognition of their value and of the power of this world-changing movement. I hope this won't be an isolated incident but that magazines around the world will finally start to highlight and give a voice to the thousands of women who are changing society for the better. The power of information and media exposure is fundamental to transforming the culture we are immersed in.

The only thing that really bothered me while reading this historic edition of *Time*, was seeing the images that accompanied these incredible women's stories corrected with Photoshop. Women of 30, 40 and 50 years appeared with skin so smooth it would be unbelievable on a 20-year-old. Why do we still insist on pretending that women do not age? Why can't we change this aesthetic dictatorship now? We have had enough of it, sincerely. I personally refuse to Photoshop my pictures, both on my Instagram profile and those that appear in magazines. It is just so wrong. We are not only our body and our body does not need to be forever perfect. We are our wrinkles; we are the signs on our skin; we are the marks of expression on our bodies, our imperfections, our age. Ageing is not a crime and women should stop being so scared of it. Unfortunately, many women over 30 are now afraid to smile in pictures in case they show their wrinkles. And many women, even my friends, are still unwilling to declare their real age. I find it so sad and I will never stop pushing them to break the psychological chains which have them bound to a culture that treats us merely as dolls. We live under a tyranny founded on an insane premise: that women's only value is superficial and youthful beauty. This is not true. Beauty is not how society has defined it and it should not be that. Our intelligence and our character are our most important features, and after them comes beauty. I hope that the younger generations will understand this and I try to be an example to them as best as I can.

The beauty of the #MeToo movement is that, while it began with a Hollywood-centric scandal, it has ended up having consequences in many other workplaces, such as Silicon Valley start-ups, hospitals, universities, media networks, political parties and governments etc. It has revealed to us the incredible ubiquity of this detestable and criminal behaviour throughout the developed and developing world. Susan Fowler has been named 'Person of the Year' by the *Financial Times*. She is the software engineer who lifted the lid on sexual harassment at Uber and inspired women to speak out by posting a blog about the year she spent working there. She revealed that her boss had propositioned her for sex on the very first day she joined his team. This behaviour was just the norm in the Uber universe, and the culture of harassment was being fostered by the indifference and tolerance of the staff and management. Ms Fowler told the *Financial Times* that, 'Women have been speaking up for many, many years, but were very rarely believed, and there were almost never any real consequences for offenders. This year, that completely changed.' Fortunately, her blog post generated an avalanche effect that brought with it the removal of Travis Kalanick as CEO, who was considered guilty by his investors of creating a company whose culture had become poisonous.

Finally we are punishing harassers. Bill O'Reilly, the former Fox News host, faced the same destiny as Kalanick when he was accused by his fellow anchor Megyn Kelly of having sexually harassed her for years. As so often seems to be the case with men found guilty of such misdemeanours, O'Reilly was in fact a serial offender and in the wake of Kelly's accusation many other women finally found the courage to speak up. I particularly like the words of Wendy Walsh, a psychologist and former guest of Fox News: 'I felt it was my duty, as a mother of daughters, as an act of love for women everywhere and the women who are silenced, to be brave.' This is what all of us should do. This is a real revolution, real sisterhood.

So why now? There are many reasons for why this is happening now, and it can to some extent be seen as part of the natural evolution of female empowerment in Western countries, but most explanations point to the presence of Donald Trump, a sexual predator, in the White House. He was even caught on record boasting about sexually assaulting women. In a 2005 recording that was released shortly before his election, Mr Trump says, 'When you're a star, they let you do it. You can do anything ... Grab 'em by the pussy. You can do anything.' Since then, at least 16 women have come forward to accuse Mr Trump of sexual harassment. The fact that he was elected to the highest office despite those remarks has fuelled a backlash not only in the USA but all over the world. The day after his inauguration, millions of women across hundreds of cities, including London, took to the streets to demonstrate in the Women's March. The stateside marches were the largest mass protest in US history. This was an unprecedented moment when women, seemingly helpless in the face of such a monstrous misogynist's victory, rose up and took back their power and self-respect by speaking out and showing their emotions. I really hope this will be a lesson learnt; one that will encourage women to finally start voting other women into power and to try and create that critical mass of female leaders that will make the difference. Paradoxically, Mr Trump's misogyny is boosting the feminist movement all over the world. We know that one day he will go home, powerless, but that feminism will continue growing until we reach real equality with complete and utter respect for women's rights. There is always light after the dark.

7
Bonus Care Draft Bill

'I want to give women the power, since they are agents of economic change. The end of extreme poverty is at hand.'

Melinda Gates

In Italy, as in many other countries, the main hindrance to women's employment is the difficulty faced in combining family and professional life. The problem has cultural and structural roots related to the unbalanced distribution of domestic work burdening women and the lack of full-time nurseries and schools. Hence, after pregnancy, the number of employed women decreases dramatically.

In the 15-49 age group, the employment rate is falling for all women; not only for the younger ones, who still live with their parents and are worst affected by the economic crisis, but also for single women and for those who have a partner. The crisis has worsened new mothers' condition in the job market, reversing the improving trend recorded between 2000 and 2005. The women who are most exposed to the risk of quitting or losing their jobs are new mothers who used to work on fixed-term contracts (45.7 per cent in 2002).

Women's employment and maternity
In Western countries, women's employment prospects directly affect the birth rate. Discrimination against women within the world of work, and the consequent frustration they feel at having to give up on their aspirations, leads to a drop in their fertility rate, and, as a result, in the birth

rate. That is why Italy is among the countries with acute problems posed by an ageing population.

In 2012, we had 148.6 people aged over 65 for every 100 under 14. In the mid-1990s, the ratio was 112 to 100. The situation is bound to get worse. According to forecasts, in 2059 we will have 263 elderly people for every 100 young people. If we consider the state of women's employment and the diminishing birth rate, the future of our country is no longer sustainable. We need to act structurally to bring an end to this catch-22 situation which is leading Italy to collapse.

International data

Women's employment rate variation in Europe between 2008 and 2013 (ISTAT data):

Germany	+7.0%
Belgium	+4.8%
Austria	+4.5%
Sweden	+3.0%
United Kingdom	+2.5%
Italy	**-0.1%**
Spain	-10.6%
Portugal	-10.7%
Greece	-18.4%

Employment rate of women with children in Europe:

Sweden	78%
France	65%
Germany	57%
United Kingdom	57%
Italy	**54%**

Global Gender Gap Index 2013 (World Economic Forum):

> Italy: 71st out of 136 countries in terms of gender gap
> Italy: 97th out of 136 countries in terms of women's participation in economic life

Global Gender Gap Index 2014 (World Economic Forum):

> Italy: 69th out of 142 countries in terms of gender gap
> Italy: 114th out of 142 countries in terms of women's participation in economic life

In 2014, Italy moved up two positions in the overall ranking, but moved down substantially in comparison with the economic-life ranking of the previous year: from 97th to 114th place. One of the worst indexes refers to 'wage equality for similar work': Italy came in 129th place (in 2014 a woman earned 48 per cent of a man's average salary). Yasmina Bekhouche, co-author of the World Economic Forum report, argues that Italy's placing is explained by women's low employment rate: only 47 per cent of women are employed, compared to 74 per cent of men.

Obstacles to 'Womenomics'

In Italy 'Womenomics' is stuck basically as a result of three structural flaws in our culture: the disproportionate amount of domestic work done by women; the ongoing prejudices against women's employment; and a lack of the so-called 'reconciliation' policies (combining work and family life) needed on both a national and local level and mainly within companies.

When we look at domestic and professional work globally, women's working hours are almost double men's (based on the average weekly hours throughout their lifespan), with a significant peak during their children's very early years, when a woman works five times more hours than her partner.

This inequality in working hours comes at a very high cost for Italian society, especially if we consider the public education expenses for unemployed women graduates. Although in Italy the percentage of women graduates has exceeded that of men graduates since 2001, four years after graduation 23 per cent of women are still unemployed compared to just 14.8 per cent of men (ISTAT 2011). Besides, five years after their degree, women earn roughly 30 per cent less than their male peers, under the same conditions.

The cost of welfare

In our country, families bear most of the cost of welfare. Despite average expenses of €667 per month, just 31.4 per cent of families benefit from some kind of state subsidy, and this is mainly apportioned to the families of elderly disabled people (19.9 per cent). As the expenses incurred by those in need affect 29.5 per cent of family income, it is not surprising that today, during the global recession, 56.4 per cent of Italians cannot cope with it and take severe measures: 48.2 per cent of them reduce their consumption of food and other necessities in order to keep a domestic helper, 20.2 per cent draw on their savings and 2.8 per cent fall into debt. 15 per cent of families (20 per cent in the North) are calling on a member of the family to give up work to replace domestic helpers. 25 per cent of families with a non-self-sufficient person and no domestic helper, rely on a young (66 per cent of them are less than 44) woman (90.4 per cent of the cases) who quit her job (9.7 per cent), or significantly reduced her hours (8.6 per cent), or simply gave up looking for one (6.7 per cent).

Within the OECD, Italy is the country with the highest percentage of families taking care of elderly or disabled people (16.2 per cent of the population; twice that of Sweden). Nowadays, a significant number of families are forced to informally hire carers themselves, paying them out of their own pockets, often off the books, and with no guarantees as to their professionalism or reliability.

Public welfare has been reduced. The increase in life expectancy, the ageing population and the forecasts of ever greater numbers of disabled and non-self-sufficient people highlight the growing need for social protection. In the years to come, the pressure on the health services will create demands that cannot be met. More and more care workers will have to be employed as the average age of the population rises. ISTAT 2007-2015 estimates show that at the end of the reference period, Italians over 65 will number 13,244,915, equal to 21.5 per cent of the population. Among them:

- 6,714,937 citizens over 75
- 1,915,111 citizens over 85
- 25,792 citizens over 100

It has been estimated that over 2.7 million of these people will have problems limiting their self-sufficiency, and will need assistance. In order to improve women's employment, family 'self-handling' must be replaced with appropriate support services, as experience in Italy and all over Europe has shown. The grandmother's role will become more and more difficult to perform, thus undermining a welfare model that relies on close family members' mutual help. Grandmothers will be burdened by their longer-lasting jobs, by taking care of their grandchildren, by their own domestic work and by looking after elderly and non-self-sufficient parents.

Within domestic life, we need to take into account a high rate of both partially and entirely undeclared work. Today, it is thought that such data affects 62 per cent of an estimated 1,655,000 domestic helpers (CENSIS AND ACLI-Colf data). The figures for undeclared work are imprecise, however, since in most cases both parties – the employer and the employee – have no interest in making it publicly known. In a few cases, such a working relationship is registered to ensure some sort of legality but both parties are encouraged to declare the minimum working hours required by law.

Bonus Care Draft Bill

In order to accord with Article 3 of the Constitution – 'All citizens have equal social dignity and are equal before the law, without distinction of sex, race, language, religion, political opinion, personal and social conditions. It is the duty of the Republic to remove those obstacles of an economic or social nature which constrain the freedom and equality of citizens, thereby impeding the full development of the human person and the effective participation of all workers in the political, economic and social organisation of the country' – and to support and sustain women's employment, some tax measure must be implemented. My proposition is for an 80 per cent annual tax allowance for workers: either female employees, women entrepreneurs or self-employed women who hire domestic helpers on contracts. The term 'domestic helpers' refers to those in charge of household care, childcare and the elderly (cleaning ladies, babysitters, carers). Tax allowances should apply from the date the bill comes into force and be available over the following ten years. Italy has one of the lowest women's employment rates in Europe, higher only than that of Greece and Malta. Such an imbalance burdens the development of the country. Women's employment fosters income and wealth, and it seems to have been the main engine of growth in the world economy over recent decades. The details of my proposed draft bill are as follows:

Aims:
- support for families
- increased opportunities for women to combine work and family lives
- improvement of the female employment rate from the current 47.5 per cent to the percentage expected by the Lisbon Treaty (60 per cent). Resultant increase in birth rate as it is strictly connected to women's employment
- reduction of tax and contributory avoidance within the domestic sector. Declaring undeclared work by introducing helpers' fiscal code in employers' tax return
- increase of GNP and consumption and resultant reduction of deflation: women who work and earn a salary tend to prioritise spending their income on goods and services
- poverty risk reduction: a family with a double income is less exposed to the effects of the economic crisis

Costs:
- the bill comes at no cost since the value generated recoups its investment

Length:
- ten years, with a three-year test phase to demonstrate its economic and social benefits

Draft clauses

'Allowances for working women: with effect from the 2019 tax period and for the following nine tax periods, an amount equivalent to 80 per cent of domestic helpers' gross salaries is deducted from working women's gross tax, with due regard for relevant contractual, tax, social insurance and contribution obligations provided for in the legislation in force.'

Target groups:

The tax allowance applies to working women who hire domestic helpers. The allowance can also apply – at 100 per cent – to single, divorced or widowed fathers who support children classified as minors.

Current legislation:

The proposal is an alternative to the current legislation, where non-compatible (see Law No140/92). Allowances currently in force cannot be combined with those of the bill by members of the same family.

Restrictions:

The tax allowance only applies to one full-time or two part-time domestic help contracts. The percentage of tax deductible is in accordance with that specified in the following income brackets:

- 80 per cent of the tax due on annual incomes between €8,000 and €15,000
- 50 per cent of the tax due on annual incomes between €15,001 and €28,000
- 12 per cent of the tax due on annual incomes between €28,001 and €55,000
- 7.5 per cent of the tax due on annual incomes between €55,001 and €75,000

The allowance should not apply to annual incomes over €75,000.

Tax regulation costs:
Estimated loss in revenues: €1,830,422,190.46

Bill effects on the tax system

2.6 million families benefit from services within the National Labour Collective Agreement, 10.4 per cent of all families in Italy (ACLI-Colf and CENSIS data), but there is a lot of undeclared work.

Let us assume that just 46.5 per cent of these families register an unemployed woman. Working women, potential beneficiaries of the legislation, could be as many as 1,209,000.

In terms of tax evasion, contributions are paid on only 42.4 of every 100 hours worked by a domestic helper. Almost six working hours out of ten are therefore deprived of any kind of social-security cover (ACLI-Colf and CENSIS data).

It has been estimated that 1,026,100 domestic helpers carry out undeclared work but, since we are talking about jobs not declared officially, the amount could be higher (ACLI-Colf and CENSIS data).

Let us take the latest annual increase recorded by ISTAT and assume a 0.5-percentage-point increase in women's employment in 12 months' time, during a possible economic-recovery stage. That would lead to an increase in women's employment equal to 800,000 units per year, at least.

Let us assume that a contribution comes from these employed women and from those who keep working despite their family's domestic help needs. The average personal income tax estimated for domestic helpers amounts to €2,691 (based on an average monthly income of €900 and a 23 per cent personal income tax rate). The average personal income tax estimated for a working woman amounts to €5,265 (according to ISTAT data, a woman in Italy earns an average net salary of €1,300, with a personal income tax rate of 27 per cent). Hence, the measure is entirely paid back even when using the lowest possible assumptions for our projection. Over the course of the next ten years, the sum total of the bill's financial coverage and increased revenues has been estimated at €6,973,235,100.

Bonus Care Draft Bill: conclusion

The Bonus Care proposal for tax legislation is simple and innovative, and would encourage national growth. It would lead to affirmative action, enabling women to enter or stay within the job market. Such action is undoubtedly necessary, given the extremely low rate of women's employment in Italy.

The outcome of such legislation would be entirely positive. On social grounds it would clearly benefit our cause, and from an economic perspective the elevated rate of return on investment would be welcomed as a highly profitable result.

Bonus Care encourages undeclared work to turn into legal work, ensuring higher national tax revenues which are useful for financing subsidies. Today, almost 80 per cent of domestic-help contracts are paid by the earners of the highest income within the family – mostly husbands – therefore all the new contracts under the bill (from 1 January 2019) will foster tax-revenue growth as well as incentives to women's employment and to the creation of new jobs.

It is 'win-win' tax legislation, since revenue will grow more than contributions. Services will create more services: double-income families will act as producers of economic activities and jobs. 'Womenomics' will foster growth within consumption and services and will lead to investment and innovation, boosting the development of the whole economic system.

The bill will produce a strong positive effect in fiscal terms since it encourages the disclosure of the majority of undeclared work within the domestic help sector. It will discourage those women who are willing to benefit from the legislation from attempting tax avoidance and evasion: they will have to declare compatible incomes. Women who think of quitting their jobs after pregnancy will be encouraged to continue their careers, since they will now be able to deduct domestic-help costs almost entirely. Women with elderly relatives to look after will also be able to continue working.

Once women's employment has been embraced, it will produce more consumption and more revenue for the country in terms of tax contributions. If the level of women's employment rose from the current 47 per cent to 60 per cent, GNP would increase by 7 per cent, according to the Bank of Italy.

Another important effect will be an increase in fertility and the resultant rise in the birth rate – both key factors in growth and sustainability in a country with one of the oldest populations in the world. A greater degree of economic self-sufficiency will encourage carefully planned family units.

'Womenomics' will contribute to the development of the entire economic system. We can create up to 15 extra jobs within the service industry for every 100 women entering the world of work. Let us remember how valuable the long-term social effects of women's employment are: economically self-sufficient women provided with a social role are less exposed to financial problems in case of divorce or adversity; they are more fulfilled and enjoy a greater sense of well-being which they can pass on to their children, helping create a better society.

An overall expansion of women's employment would help eliminate 'new poverty': unemployed young couples suffering from economic deprivation who are forced to go back and live with their parents, becoming a drain on parental resources or even on older relatives' pensions. The bill would have a beneficial impact on the middle classes, who have been hit the hardest by the crisis. It would directly act to better women's circumstances, and by doing so come to the aid of entire family units and society as a whole. Provided renovation costs are deducted, is it not time to allow cost reductions in household management for those who have always been burdened with such a heavy load?

ACKNOWLEDGEMENTS

Thank you to all the beautiful minds that have inspired me during the last ten years. And to all the people who have discriminated against me or made me feel uncomfortable, because your nastiness has made me stronger and more resolute. Many thanks to all my real friends who support me every day, especially my Sorority sisters who made me feel right at home when I arrived in London. I'm so grateful to all of you, but to name just a few: Geeta Siddhu-Robb, Selma Day, Maki Aboofazeli, Ching He Huang, Victoria Christian, Sarah Ho, Orla Constant, Lisa Tze, Shelley Von Strunckel and Tessy Nassau. I feel blessed. Real sisterhood does exist. And, of course, I'd like to thank my family: my talented children, who have made me a better woman and for whom I keep fighting to forge a better world, and my mother, whose strength is a true marvel. Life is an incredibly beautiful journey if you are in good company and surrounded by love.